Beyond Basic
KNITTING

0 11557 03489 9

Beyond Basic
KNITTING

Techniques and Projects to Expand Your Skills

Leigh Ann Berry, editor

Anita J. Tosten and Missy Burns,
knitters and consultants

Photographs by
Alan Wycheck

Illustrations by
David Bienkowski

STACKPOLE
BOOKS

Copyright © 2008 by Stackpole Books

Published by
STACKPOLE BOOKS
5067 Ritter Road
Mechanicsburg, PA 17055
www.stackpolebooks.com

Printed in China

10 9 8 7 6 5 4 3 2 1

First edition

The twice-worked bind off used in the Lantz Corners Shawl (page 51) is the creation of Judy Pascale.

The first 30 rounds of the Lantz Corners Shawl are taken from James Norbury's *Traditional Knitting Patterns from Scandinavia, the British Isles, France, Italy and other European Countries* (Dover Publications, 1973).

Library of Congress Cataloging-in-Publication Data

Beyond basic knitting : techniques and projects to expand your skills / Leigh Ann Berry, editor ; Anita J. Tosten and Missy Burns, knitters and consultants ; photographs by Alan Wycheck ; illustrations by David Bienkowski. — 1st ed.
        p. cm.
ISBN-13: 978-0-8117-3489-9
ISBN-10: 0-8117-3489-7
1. Knitting. I. Berry, Leigh Ann.
TT820.B63 2008
746.43'2—dc22
                                                         2008005691

Contents

Acknowledgments

A lot has happened since I first signed on to do the *Beyond Basic Knitting* project. Shortly after I agreed to do the book, I found out that I was expecting my first child, Quentin, who was born in December 2006. His arrival, while joyous, nevertheless eliminated what little free time I had and made finding time to work on the book project a challenge. To that end, I owe an immense debt of gratitude to my husband, Garrick. It was only with his help and support that I was able to complete the project.

I am also deeply grateful to my contributors, Missy Burns and Anita Tosten, both of whom lent their time and talent to the projects featured in the book. Anita's creativity is evident in all ten of the designs, and her expertise forms the basis of many of the tips and Skill Workshops throughout the book. Missy's organizational skill and attention to detail helped to make the logistics of writing the patterns and delivering the projects run smoothly. It has been my pleasure and honor to work with them on this second project.

Alan Wycheck's talent with the camera is evident on just about every page of this book. His eye for capturing both the minutiae of close-up skill shots and the styling of the model photos makes him an integral part of Stackpole's Basics series.

My thanks to my fellow series author Sharon Silverman for generously sharing her illustrator David Bienkowski with me for this project. David's skill at producing a computer-generated version of Alan's photographs helped to illustrate several of the more complex skills throughout the book.

Thanks also to Melanie Wagner, Sarah Wycheck and Regan Schnell, who modeled the garments for the book, and to Frank and Terrie Albano, who graciously allowed us to use their beautiful home and property for the photo shoot. My thanks also to Trish McKinney, owner of the Yarn Gallery in Reading, PA, who was able to help by miraculously producing two skeins of otherwise unobtainable yarn I needed to finish one of the projects.

Finally, my most sincere thanks to Janelle Steen, Mark Allison, and Judith Schnell at Stackpole Books, who have been with me every step of the way with this project. Janelle has masterfully managed the details of the publication process from manuscript to finished book. In the face of unforeseen challenges and delays, Mark's patience and flexibility have made my job much easier. I am especially grateful to Judith, who, both as an editor and as a friend, continues to be a support to me.

Introduction

*B*eyond Basic Knitting assumes that the reader has a moderate amount of experience with the craft. Therefore, skills such as executing the basic knit and purl stitches, checking gauge, joining new yarn, weaving in new stitches, and blocking are mentioned, but not explained. For a thorough explanation of these skills, please see *Basic Knitting: All the Tools and Skills You Need to Get Started* (Stackpole, 2004).

What you will find in this book is a brief review of some intermediate skills as well as an introduction to more advanced techniques that you can add to your repertoire. The true focus of the book is the projects section that will highlight these advanced techniques and show how they are applied in a particular project. The Skill Workshops throughout the book each focus on an individual technique and provide in-depth explanations on how to apply them. The Project in Progress sections take an in-depth look at a particularly complex aspect of a project and guide you through step by step.

The projects in the book are not arranged by level of difficulty, and are independent of one another. You can select whatever type of project suits your fancy without worrying about missing any of the skills in previous projects.

So browse through and see which of the ten projects you want to try out first. Then head out to your local yarn shop for supplies, pick up your needles, and get started!

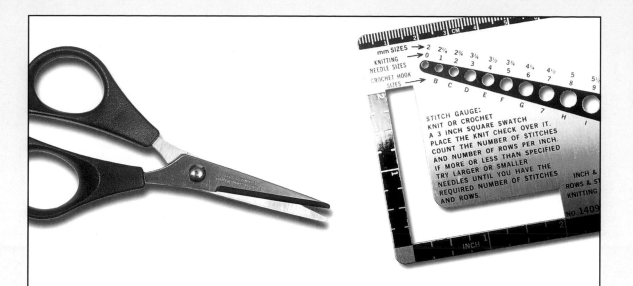

Part I

Materials and Basic Skills Review

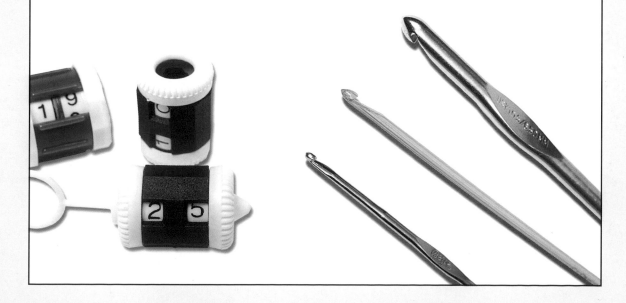

Materials

Yarn

WEIGHT

In order to provide a measure of consistency in yarn labeling, the Craft Yarn Council of America (CYCA) has issued a set of standards dealing with yarn weight. The guidelines organize yarn into six main weight categories ranging from Super Fine (1) up to Super Bulky (6). In between are Fine (2), Light (3), Medium (4), and Bulky (5). See the appendix on page 114 for more details on this organizational structure.

The CYCA's 6 yarn weight categories (from top to bottom): Super Fine, Fine, Light, Medium, Bulky, and Super Bulky.

COMPOSITION AND STRUCTURE

The vast majority of knitting yarn is created by spinning fibers together. Fibers can be natural, such as wool or mohair, silk or cotton; man-made, such as acrylic, nylon or polyester; or a blend of the two. Each fiber has its own distinctive characteristics and properties, some of which are desirable and others which are less so. Wool, for example, is extremely warm, but is not as strong as other fibers. Acrylic, on the other hand, is extremely durable, but does not breathe well. Sometimes a blend of the two materials maximizes the advantages of each. For example, a sock yarn made of a 92% wool and 8% nylon blend provides the warmth and comfort of natural wool with the added strength and resilience of synthetic fiber.

The way in which the yarn's fibers are spun together determines its structure. There are a variety of different yarn structures:

Spiral: A thinner yarn twisted around a thicker yarn.

Chenille: A velvety pile, wrapped with two thin, twisted threads. Can be either long-pile or short-pile.

Bouclé: Two strands twisted at varying tensions, held together with a thin binding thread to produce loops of yarn.

Nubby: Two strands twisted so that one overlaps another to produce a bumpy texture.

Slubby: A strand that is alternately thick and thin, twisted with either a smooth or a slubby second strand.

Tape: Yarn made of knitted threads and woven into a narrow, flat band.

Novelty Yarns: Most common types combine metallic threads or feature long "eyelash" textures.

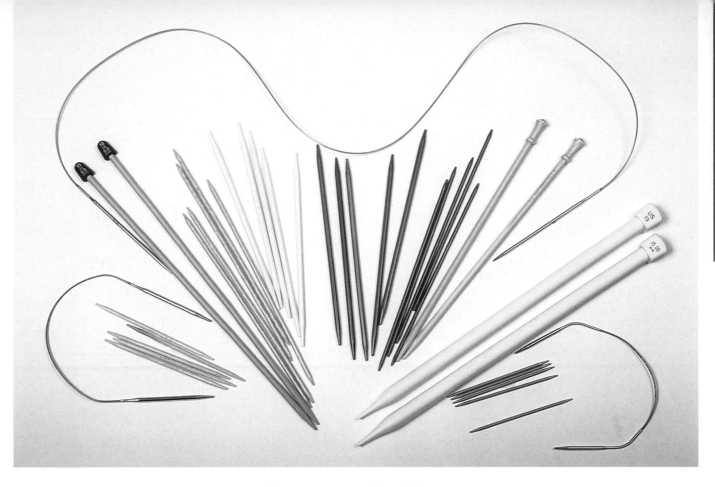

Knitting Needle Sizes[*]

Millimeter Range	U.S. Size Range
2.25 mm	1
2.75 mm	2
3.25 mm	3
3.5 mm	4
3.75 mm	5
4 mm	6
4.5 mm	7
5 mm	8
5.5 mm	9
6 mm	10
6.5 mm	10$\frac{1}{2}$
8 mm	11
9 mm	13
10 mm	15
12.75 mm	17
15 mm	19
19 mm	35
25 mm	50

From the Craft Yarn Council of America's Standards and Guidelines for Crochet and Knitting

Needles

Needles come in three main varieties: straight, circular, or double pointed. They range in both length and size from a 2.25 mm size 1 needle up to a 25 mm size 50 needle. They also come in a range of different materials: aluminum, steel, plastic, bamboo, or wood. The last two materials are typically more expensive, but can be more pleasurable to knit with.

Materials

Other Equipment

Materials

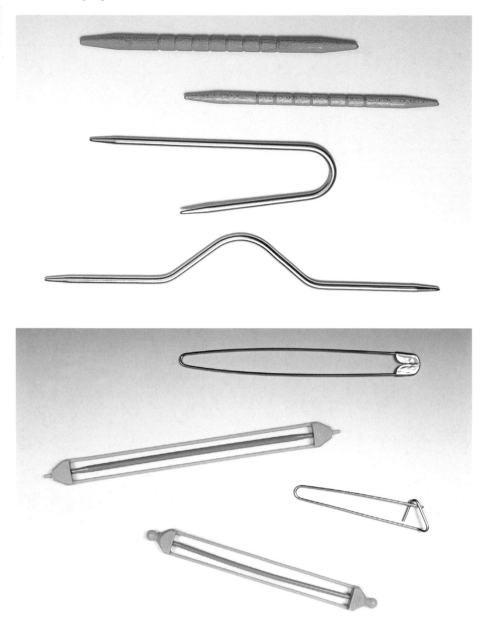

CABLE NEEDLES
Used to hold stitches when working cables.

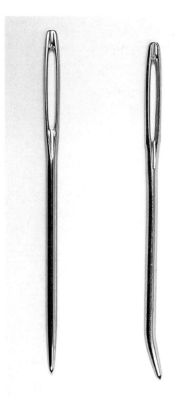

TAPESTRY NEEDLES
Used in finishing to sew up seams and run in ends. They come in both straight and bent-tipped varieties.

STITCH HOLDERS
Used to temporarily hold a group of stitches while continuing to knit others.

SMALL SCISSORS
Used to cut yarn.

CROCHET HOOKS

Used to correct mistakes by rescuing dropped stitches or to create trims and accents in finishing.

ROW COUNTERS

Used to keep track of rows as you knit. They slip over a single-pointed needle for easy access.

STITCH MARKERS

Used to slip over needle to indicate groups of stitches or the start of a round of circular knitting. Split markers can be used to indicate placement of seams or individual stitches.

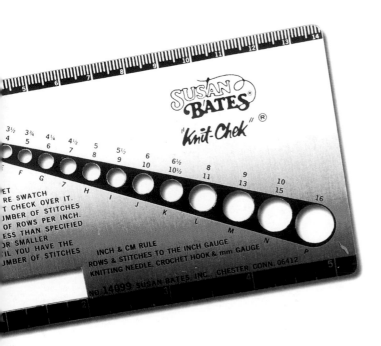

NEEDLE/STITCH GAUGE

Used to check gauge of knitted swatch as well as to confirm size of unknown knitting needles.

5

Skills

Casting On

In addition to the basic knitting-on cast-on, there are several other cast-ons that can be used in specific patterns.

THE LONG-TAIL CAST-ON
For garments such as sweaters, socks, or hats that require a more elastic edge, the long-tail cast-on is a better choice than the basic method. In this method, you estimate how much yarn will be required for the cast-on stitches, leaving enough yarn for an adequate tail.

1. Estimate how much yarn you need for your tail by simply wrapping the yarn around the needle: one wrap for each stitch to be cast on. Add an additional 3-inch length of yarn to run in later.

2. Unwrap the loops and use that length as the tail. Make a slip knot.

3. Holding the needle with the loop on it in your right hand, let the working yarn and tail hang straight down from the needle, with the working yarn behind the tail. Hold the thumb and index finger of your left hand together.

4. Insert your thumb and index finger in between the two dangling pieces of yarn.

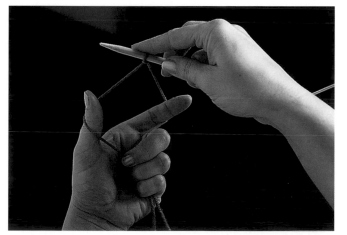

5. Pull the needle toward you, wrapping the working yarn clockwise around your left index finger and the tail counterclockwise around your thumb. (This process looks a lot like making a slingshot.)

6. Draw both ends into your palm and hold them down with your remaining fingers. The needle in your right hand and your left hand with the yarn should be straight up and down, with a little slack between the two.

7. Push the needle up through the loop on your thumb from the bottom.

8. Catch the working yarn on your index finger and draw it down through the loop.

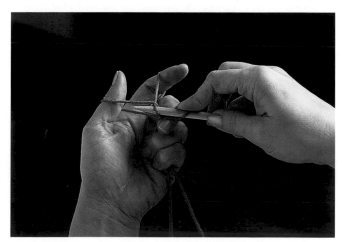

9. Pull the working yarn through the loop.

10. Release the loop of yarn from your thumb, gently pulling down on the tail with your thumb to tighten the loop.

Stitches cast on by the long-tail method

Tip: This method produces a cast-on that is smooth on the front and bumpy on the back. Because of this, it is necessary that you make the first row of your knitting a wrong-side row (for example, if you are knitting in stockinette stitch, start with a purl row rather than a knit row).

11. Continue pulling down with your thumb until the loop is snug on the needle.

Tip: Don't let go of the yarn in your palm. Make sure when you rewrap the yarn around your thumb that you wrap counter-clockwise.

THE CABLE CAST-ON
This method produces a sturdy but elastic edge that is ideal for use with ribbing.

12. Reposition the yarn on your thumb and index finger and repeat Steps 6–11 until you have the required number of stitches.

1. Cast on two stitches on the left needle using the basic knitting-on cast-on.

4. Place the new stitch back on the left needle.

5. Repeat Steps 2 and 3 to cast on the required number of stitches.

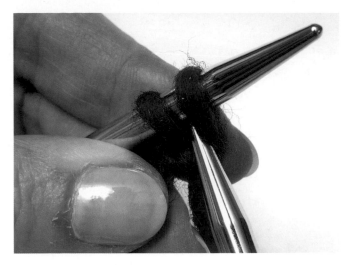

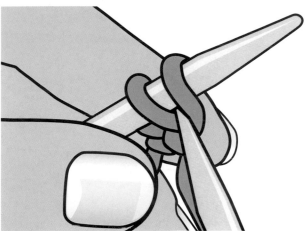

2. Insert the right needle between the two stitches on the left needle.

A finished row of cable cast-on stitches

3. Wrap the yarn around the right needle as if to knit and pull the stitch through.

Shaping

This section will review just a few of the most common increases and decreases. Consult *Basic Knitting* for a full description of the range of methods available.

Increases

MAKE ONE (M1)
This increase is commonly used in shaping garments. In this method, the increase is worked into the "ladder" between the two stitches from the previous row of knitting. Two different versions of the increase, the right slant and the left slant, are typically used in conjunction with one another to provide a symmetrical increase.

MAKE ONE (LEFT SLANT)

1. On a knit row of your swatch, knit to the point in the row that you want to work the increase. Before knitting the next stitch, gently spread the needles apart. Notice the strand of yarn that bridges the gap between these two stitches.

2. Insert the tip of the left needle (not the right needle) from front to back under this "ladder" and lift it onto the left needle.

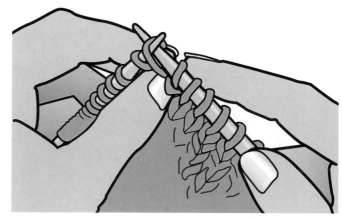

3. Insert the tip of the right needle through the back of the stitch.

10

4. Knit the stitch.

5. Slide the new stitch off the needle and knit the rest of the row as usual.

An M1 (left slant) increase on a knit side row

To work this increase on a purl row:

1. Purl to the point in the row that you want to work the increase. Before purling the next stitch, gently spread the needles apart. Notice the strand of yarn that bridges the gap between these two stitches.

2. Insert the tip of the left needle from front to back under this "ladder" and lift it onto the left needle.

3. Insert the tip of the right needle through the back of the stitch.

4. Purl the stitch.

5. Slide the new stitch off the needle and purl the rest of the row as usual.

An M1 (left slant) increase on a purl side row as seen from the right side of the piece

MAKE ONE (RIGHT SLANT)

1. On a knit row of your swatch, knit to the point in the row that you want to work the increase. Before knitting the next stitch, gently spread the needles apart. Notice the strand of yarn that bridges the gap between these two stitches.

2. Insert the tip of the left needle (not the right needle) from back to front under this "ladder" and lift it onto the left needle.

3. Insert the tip of the right needle through the front of the stitch.

4. Knit the stitch.

5. Slide the new stitch off the needle and knit the rest of the row as usual.

An M1 (right slant) increase on a knit side row

To work this increase on a purl row:

1. Purl to the point in the row that you want to work the increase. Before purling the next stitch, gently spread the needles apart. Notice the strand of yarn that bridges the gap between these two stitches.

2. Insert the tip of the left needle from back to front under this "ladder" and lift it onto the left needle.

3. Insert the tip of the right needle through the front of the stitch.

4. Purl the stitch.

5. Slide the new stitch off the needle and purl the rest of the row as usual.

An M1 (right slant) increase on a purl side row as seen from the right side of the piece

Decreases

KNIT 2 TOGETHER (K2TOG)

This right-slanting decrease is usually used in conjunction with its mirror image, the left-slanting slip slip knit decrease (ssk—see page 15). A common use is in shaping a sock.

1. On a knit row of your swatch, knit to the point in the row that you want to work the decrease.

2. Insert the right needle into the next two stitches at the same time, as to knit.

Needle inserted into both stitches as to knit

3. Knit the two stitches together.

4. Slide the stitch onto the right needle and knit the rest of the row as usual.

A k2tog decrease on a knit side row

SLIP, SLIP, KNIT (SSK)
This is a subtle, left-slanting decrease.

1. On a knit row of your swatch, knit to the point in the row that you want to work the decrease.

2. Slip the next two stitches in the row by inserting the tip of your right needle into them as if to knit, but instead slide them onto the right needle without knitting them.

Both stitches slipped as if to knit

3. Insert the tip of the left needle into the front of the two slipped stitches to hold them in place.

4. Knit the stitches together through the backs with the right needle.

5. Slide the two stitches off the left needle and knit the rest of the row as usual.

An ssk decrease from a knit side row

Other Stitches

C2B (CROSS 2 BACK) (*Used in Sugar Run Skirt, page 31*)

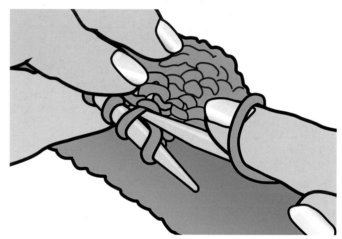

1. Knit into the back of the second stitch on the left-hand needle.

2. Knit into front of the first stitch on the left-hand needle.

3. Slip both stitches off the needle at the same time.

Several C2B stitches stacked on top of one another

Binding Off

In addition to learning the basic bind off, this technique is useful when joining seams.

The 3-Needle Bind Off

The 3-needle bind off provides the ideal way to join together two identical seams smoothly and evenly. When using this technique, the stitches should still be on the needles (or on a stitch holder) and each needle must have the same number of stitches as the other one.

1. Place the two right sides of the garment together, with the stitches to be joined still on the needles and the stitch holder. Hold the needle and the holder parallel.

Tip: Make sure to use a large stitch holder so you will have plenty of room to knit from it.

2. Insert a third needle into the first two stitches (one on the needle and one on the stitch holder) as if to knit.

3. Knit the two stitches together. You should have one stitch on the right needle.

4. Repeat Step 2 with the next set of stitches, knitting them together as one. You will now have two stitches on the right needle.

5. Using the point of the left needle, lift the first knit stitch up and pass it over the second stitch.

6. Slide the stitch off the right needle.

7. Knit the next set of two stitches and repeat Steps 5 and 6 to bind off the next set of stitches on the right needle.

8. Continue binding off until you are left with only one stitch on your right needle.

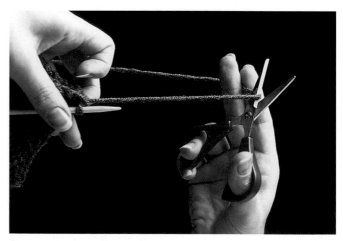

9. Cut the working yarn, leaving a 3-inch tail, and pull the cut end through the final stitch to finish off.

The shoulder seam from the right side of the garment

Finishing

Making I-cord

I-cord is a name first coined by knitting pioneer Elizabeth Zimmerman to describe easy-to-knit, decorative cording that has a multitude of uses in knitting projects. According to her daughter, Meg Swansen, the original technique was actually called "idiot cord," but Zimmerman "thought the name rather rude" and shortened it to "I-cord." See Elizabeth Zimmerman's classic book, *Knitting Workshop* (see the Resources section on page 115 for publication details), for many more creative applications for I-cord.

I-cord is incredibly easy to make:

1. Cast on 3, 4, 5, or even 6 stitches (depending on how wide you want your I-cord to be) using the cable method on double pointed needles.

2. Knit across the first row but do not turn.

3. Slide the stitches to the opposite end of the needle.

4. Knit the next row as usual, from right to left. Pull the working yarn taut against the needle to avoid any gaps.

5. Repeat Steps 2–4 until your I-cord reaches the desired length.

Kitchener Stitch

The best way to join together two open edges of knitted stitches is to weave them together using a grafting method called Kitchener stitch. The technique is named after Lord Kitchener, who, during World War I, contributed to a sock pattern with a grafted toe for women in the United States and Canada to knit for the soldiers in the trenches.

This example illustrates how to graft stitches together at the toe of a sock using Kitchener stitch:

1. Place the wrong sides of the pieces to be grafted together and arrange the stitches on the needles so that they are parallel, with the needles pointing in the same direction.

2. Cut the working yarn, leaving an ample tail (at least twice the length of the stitches on the needles). Thread the tail through the eye of a tapestry needle.

3. Holding the needles in your left hand, with the work pushed to the end of the points facing right, draw the tapestry needle through the first stitch on the front needle as if to purl. Leave it on the needle.

6. Slip the stitch off the needle.

Tip: Keep the tension constant throughout your grafting; try to match that of the sock itself. It is better to graft too loosely than too tightly. You can always go back and tighten loose grafting before you finish the seam.

4. Now, draw the needle through the first stitch on the back needle as if to knit. Leave it on the needle.

Tip: The working yarn must pass under the needles when moving from front to back.

7. Draw the needle through the next stitch on the front needle as if to purl. Leave it on the needle.

5. Draw the needle through the first stitch on the front needle as if to knit.

8. Carrying the working yarn under the needles, draw the needle through the first stitch on the back needle as if to purl.

9. Slip the stitch off the needle.

10. Draw the needle through the next stitch on the back needle as if to knit. Leave it on the needle.

11. Repeat Steps 5–10 until you have used up all the stitches on both needles and you have a complete seam.

12. Once your seam is complete, you will need to tighten it by gently pulling the working thread from the back end of the seam to the front. Use the needle to pull the loose seam stitches tighter. Don't pull too tightly.

A finished Kitchener stitch toe seam

Knitting from a Pattern

For the beginning knitter, knitting patterns can often appear confusing. But once you know the basic information the pattern communicates and what to do with it, they make much more sense. Take a look at the Sugar Run Skirt on page 31. Each section is identified and explained below.

Tip: Make sure you read the entire sentence in the pattern before starting to knit. Sometimes patterns contain more than one instruction per sentence.

GAUGE

As discussed, gauge is crucial to proper garment fit. In this case, the gauge is expressed as 24 stitches and 32 rows = 4 inches on a size 5 needle. Knit a test swatch and test your gauge before beginning this project.

MEASUREMENTS

Most garment patterns provide a range of sizes. You will first need to obtain accurate measurements for yourself or the intended wearer and then consult the pattern's sizing chart to determine which size is most appropriate. You will then cast on the correct number of stitches required to create that size of garment. You can also refer to the body measurement tables on pages 110–113 if the pattern does not include a sizing chart.

Tip: One good way to get measurements for a knitted piece is to take a similar garment (your favorite sweater, for example) and lay it on a flat surface for measurement. Remember that the actual size of sweaters and other similar garments is measured across the widest part of the garment; length is measured from the top of the shoulder to the lower edge of the garment; and sleeve length is measured through the center of the sleeve from the shoulder seam to the cuff. Once you have the measurements of your favorite sweater, you can check them against the "actual" measurements in the pattern to see which size most closely corresponds with your ideal fit.

Once you've decided which size garment you want to knit, you will be able to determine how much yarn you will need and how many stitches you will initially need to cast on. Patterns usually use parentheses to indicate additional sizes. The main size is listed first and subsequent larger sizes are listed in parentheses following it: 32 (34, 36, 38). When reading the pattern, you need to read only the number that corresponds in sequence to the size you are knitting. In other words, a pattern will say: Cast on 64 (68, 72, 76) stitches." If you are knitting a size 36 garment, then you need to follow the second number within the brackets, or 72 stitches. Increases and decreases are also indicated in this manner, as are various other instructions such as repeating rows: "Repeat these two rows 6 (6, 8, 8) more times." It may be easier for you to read the pattern if you use a colored highlighter to indicate which numbers correspond to which size in the pattern. (If you knit the pattern again in a different size, choose a different color of highlighter.)

MATERIALS

This part of the pattern indicates which type of yarn is required for the projects. Some patterns will specify brand names of yarns while others will indicate only the type of yarn (fingering, sport, worsted) that is needed. If you are knitting a one-size garment such as a throw, a set quantity of yarn will be specified. If the pattern is for several sizes, the quantity will depend on the size you plan to knit. This section will also list any other needles and equipment, such as stitch holders, zippers, or buttons, that are needed to complete the project.

Tip: Make sure to purchase all the yarn you will need to complete your project at one time. Since yarn is usually dyed in batches, purchasing it at different times may result in having two skeins from different dye lots. The color can vary noticeably from dye lot to dye lot.

ABBREVIATIONS

Knitting patterns use abbreviations to save space when writing out instructions. Although they may seem a bit confusing at first, the more you knit the more they will become familiar. See page 109 for a list of the most common knitting abbreviations.

Asterisks (*) are often used in patterns to indicate instructions that need to be repeated. An asterisk will mark the beginning of a portion of the sequences that should be worked more than once. For example, "* k1, p1, k1, p5; rep from * to end" means that, after you've completed the sequence once, you repeat it again and again until you reach the end of the row. Brackets are also used for a similar purpose. For example, "[k1, p1] twice" means k1, p1, k1, p1.

Part II

Projects

1

Heart's Content Scarf

Gauge: 14 sts/20 rows to 4" in St st on US 10 needle (or size to obtain gauge)

Measurements: 5" x 69"

Materials:

Kid Mohair, 200 yards

Cellulose Blend, 200 yards

US 10 Needle

Sample 1 knit in Feel'n Fuzzy (90% Kid Mohair, 10% Nylon) and Gold Dust (44% Rayon, 44% Cotton, 6% Nylon, 2% Mylar)

Sample 2 knit in Feel'n Fuzzy (90% Kid Mohair, 10% Nylon) and Ladera (50% Rayon, 44% Cotton, 6% Nylon)

NOTE: Hold both yarns together throughout scarf.

On first glance it would appear that this scarf requires complicated shaping to create its unusual diagonal dimensions; however, it is actually achieved through a very simple technique known as knitting on the bias. This project introduces the technique and offers suggestions on ways it can be applied in creating other garments. The combination of delicate mohair and cellulose fiber produces a rich texture that adds to the beauty of the finished scarf. Combining different yarns is an easy way to add textural and colorful diversity to a project; this skill will be revisited in the Tionesta Lake Throw on page 93.

SCARF

CO 21 sts loosely using cable cast-on (see page 8).

PATTERN

Row 1: k1, ssk, * yo, ssk, k2; rep from * to last 2 sts, yo, k2.

Tip: Until you get into a rhythm with this pattern, it's very easy to forget this last yo. Make sure to count your stitches at the end of Row 1 to make sure you still have 21.

Row 2: Knit.
Work in pattern until piece measures 69", ending with Row 2. BO loosely.

Heart's Content Scarf

Knitting on the bias, also called diagonal knitting, is a valuable technique that can be applied to any stitch pattern. It can be used to create unusual style lines or to create an unconventional drape of a standard garment. The Heart's Content Scarf, for example, benefits from the diagonal, which adds some flair to the basic straight up-and-down scarf pattern. Bias knitting is achieved by working increases and matching decreases at either side of the garment. While the increase pushes the garment out in one direction, the decrease on the other side pulls it back in the opposite direction. The effect is a garment that grows on a slant rather than straight up and down.

You can experiment with knitting on the bias by knitting swatches that slant in opposite directions.

Bias Left Swatch

1. Using some scrap yarn (preferably a worsted weight), cast on 20 stitches. Work 4 rows of garter (gar) stitch.

2. In the next (right-side) row, knit 2 stitches, then work an ssk decrease.

Tip: See page 15 for a refresher on the ssk decrease.

3. Knit 14 stitches, then work an M1 increase.

Tip: See page 10 for a refresher on the M1 increase.

4. Knit 2 stitches to finish the row.

5. On the next (wrong-side) row, k2, p16, k2.

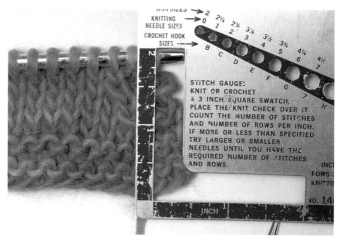

6. After a few rows, you will begin to notice that your swatch is starting to slant diagonally to the left.

7. Work Rows 1 and 2 for a total of 20 rows, then work 4 rows of garter stitch. Bind off loosely in knit.

Now try knitting a bias swatch in the opposite direction.

Bias Right Swatch

1. Cast on 20 stitches. Work 4 rows of garter stitch.

2. In the next (right-side) row, knit 2 stitches, then work an M1 increase.

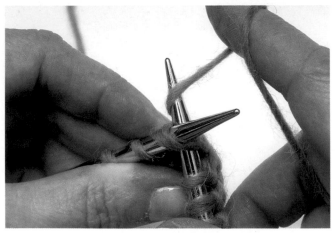

3. Knit 14 stitches, then work a k2tog decrease.

4. Knit 2 stitches to finish the row.

5. On the next (wrong-side) row, k2, p16, k2.

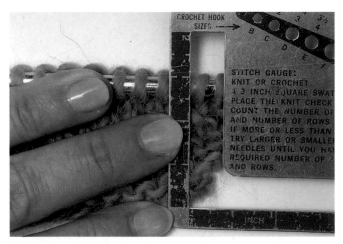

6. After a few rows, you will begin to notice that your swatch is starting to slant diagonally to the right.

7. Work Rows 1 and 2 for a total of 20 rows, then work 4 rows of garter stitch. Bind off loosely in knit.

Seeing the finished swatches side by side shows the effect of biasing.

2

Sugar Run Skirt

Gauge: 24 sts and 32 rows to 4" in St st on US 5 needles (or size to obtain gauge)

Measurements (at 1" below navel):

Finished waist: 33 (36, 39)"

Materials:

DK weight Wool/Nylon Blend **3** (200 yds/ skein), 4 (5, 6) skeins

Length of lightweight wool yarn for provisional cast-on **3**

US 5 32"–36" Circular Needle (or size to obtain gauge)

Spare 32"–36" Circular Needle, similar size (for casing)

Size G Crochet Hook

½" elastic, enough to fit snugly around waist

Samples knit in Twin Twist (92% Wool, 8% Nylon)

NOTE: Yarn choice is extremely important for this project. Look for a yarn that contains a blend of wool and nylon in order to give the skirt the stretchiness it needs. When using hand-dyed yarn, remember to vary skeins throughout to maintain color quality. In this pattern, color joins are less noticeable when worked at the C2B.

SKIRT

CO 198 (216, 234) sts using invisible cast-on: With crochet hook, chain stitch 200 (218, 236) on waste yarn. Using Twin Twist, PU 198 (216, 234) sts.

Tip: See the Skill Workshop on pages 34–35 for instructions on how to work the provisional cast-on and pick up stitches.

With bumpy side of chain showing, join (being careful not to twist stitches) and place markers as follows:

* k18, pm; rep from * around. 1st marker must be different to mark beg of round.

FIRST SET

Rnd 1: C2B, k16 around.

Tip: See page 16 for instructions on how to work the C2B.

Rnd 2 and each even rnd except Rnd 34: Knit.
Rnd 3: k1, C2B, k15 around.
Rnd 5: k2, C2B, k14 around.
Rnd 7: k3, C2B, k13 around.
Rnd 9: k4, C2B, k12 around.

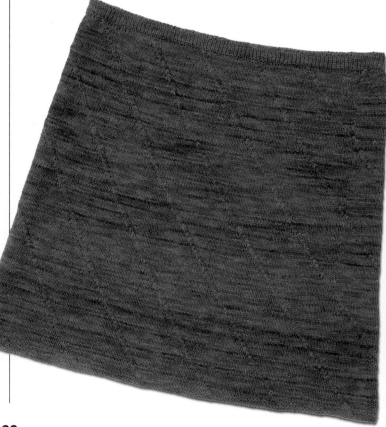

This fun project is knit with the same yarn used in the Big Rock Socks (page 80), which gives the skirt the elasticity needed to hold its shape. The shifting stitch that carries its way diagonally across the pattern provides a simple but visually interesting decorative element. This project introduces the concept of the provisional cast-on (sometimes called an invisible cast-on), that leaves "live" stitches at the top of the garment to be picked up and knit from the top of the garment up—in this case, to create the casing for the elastic at the waist of the skirt.

Rnd 11: k5, M1, C2B, k11 around—209 (228, 247) sts.

Tip: In Rnd 11, work the MI L slant as shown on page 10.

Rnd 13: k7, C2B, k10 around.

Tip: Be sure to k7 in Rnd 13 (two more than in Rnd 11).

Rnd 15: k8, C2B, k9 around.
Rnd 17: k9, C2B, k8 around.
Rnd 19: k10, C2B, k7 around.
Rnd 21: k11, C2B, k6 around.
Rnd 23: k12, C2B, k5 around.
Rnd 25: k13, C2B, k4 around.
Rnd 27: k14, C2B, k3 around.
Rnd 29: k15, C2B, k2 around.
Rnd 31: k16, C2B, k1 around.
Rnd 33: k17, C2B around.
Rnd 34: Knit to within 1 st of beg marker.
Rnd 35: Using last st from Rnd 34 and 1st st from Rnd 35, C2B being careful to move the marker correctly, k17 around to last 20 sts, C2B, k18.

Tip: When working Row 35, slip the marker off the needle with the stitches entirely and then replace it by slipping the last stitch onto the left needle momentarily, replacing the marker, then moving the last stitch back onto the right needle. Count your stitches to make sure that you have a total of 19 stitches between the two markers.

These 36 rnds form pattern.

Work 3 additional pattern sets, keeping in mind that each time you do a pattern set, you increase 1 st between each marker. This will require you to complete 2 additional rnds for each pattern set.

Tip: You should change skeins at each pattern repeat in order to ensure the color quality of the hand-dyed yarn. Remember to work in the new skein at the C2B.

SECOND SET

Work Rnds 1, 3, 5, 7, 9 as in first set, noting that each round will have one additional stitch after the C2B. (EX: Rnd 1: C2B, k17 around.)
  Rnd 2 and each even rnd except Rnd 36: Knit.
  Rnd 11: k5, M1, C2B, k12—220 (240, 260) sts.
  Work Rnds 13, 15, 17, 19, 21, 23, 25, 27, 29, 31, 33 as in first set.
  Rnd 35: k18, C2B.
  Rnd 36: Knit to within 1 st of beg marker.
  Rnd 37: Using last st from Rnd 36 and 1st st from Rnd 37, * C2B being careful to move the marker correctly, k18 around to last 21 sts, C2B, k19.

THIRD SET

  1, 3, 5, 7, 9, 11—231 (252, 273) sts, 13, 15, 17, 19, 21, 23, 25, 27, 29, 31, 33, 35, 37, 39.

FOURTH SET

  1, 3, 5, 7, 9, 11—242 (264, 286) sts, 13, 15, 17, 19, 21, 23, 25, 27, 29, 31, 33, 35, 37, 39, 41.
  Work an additional 14 rnds. Work Rnds 12 and 14 as follows:

NEXT SET

  1, 3, 5, 7, 9, 11—253 (276, 299) sts, 13.
  Rnd 12: p8, k1, p14.
  Rnd 14: p9, k1, p13.
  BO in knit.

ELASTIC CASING

PU live sts from invisible CO 1 at a time as you pull out each chain stitch 198 (216, 234) sts, pm, * k1, inc by knitting into the st below next st, knit next st; rep from * around—297 (324, 351) sts.

  For first and last size, k1 rnd inc 1 st around (298, 352) sts.

  Rnd 1: * k1, sl1 wyif; rep from * around. With 1st skein leaving yarn in front for Row 2.
  Rnd 2: * sl1 wyib, p1; rep from * around. With 2nd skein leaving yarn in back for Row 1.
  Work Rnds 1 and 2, 5x more.
  Place every other stitch on a spare needle around. You will notice that you have worked the front and back of elastic casing. Stitch ends of elastic together. Place elastic band into casing. Work Kitchener stitch with front and back casing parallel.

Tip: See the Project in Progress on page 36 for tips on how to knit the elastic casing.

Aprovisional cast-on is a method that makes use of a length of waste yarn to hold live stitches. The waste yarn is later removed and the live stitches are picked up and knit in the opposite direction. This method has a number of applications—creating a piece that is closed at both ends (such as a toy), hems, or, in this case, a waistband.

4. Turn the chain over to the back side, with the bumps visible.

1. Using a crochet hook and a length of lightweight wool, chain stitch 20 stitches.

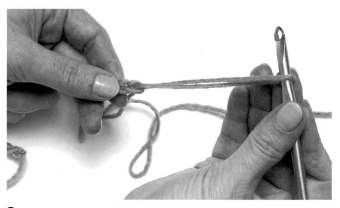

2. When you reach the end of the chain, slip the last stitch off the crochet hook and pull the loop out long to make it easy to find.

3. Tighten the loop and cut the yarn, leaving a 5-inch tail.

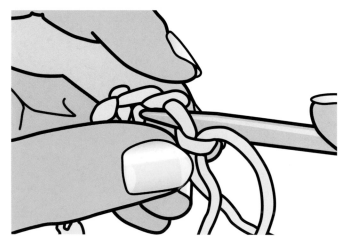

5. Insert the needle into the bump on the back side of the chain as if to purl, inserting the needle from the top to bottom of the bump.

Sugar Run Skirt

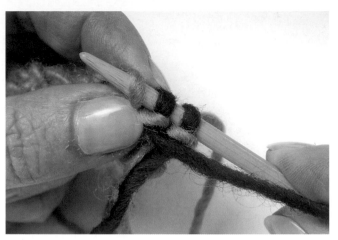

The needle with two picked-up stitches, starting to pick up the third

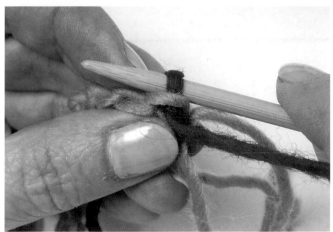

6. Loop the project yarn (blue) over the needle and pull it through, picking up a stitch.

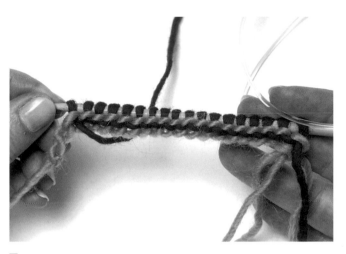

7. Repeat Step 5 to pick up 18 stitches.

Tip: Always chain stitch two more stitches than you need to cast on. (For example, in the skirt project you will chain stitch 200 stitches to pick up the 198 required for the cast-on.)

Knitting the Casing

To knit the casing for the elastic at the waist of the skirt, you will need to pick up the live stitches at the top that you first created with the invisible cast on. These stitches will form the front of the casing. You will create another complete set of stitches that will form the back of the casing, and, by adding a second skein of yarn, you will knit the front and back at the same time (called double knitting).

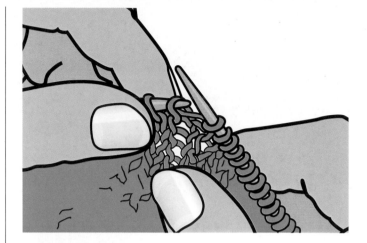

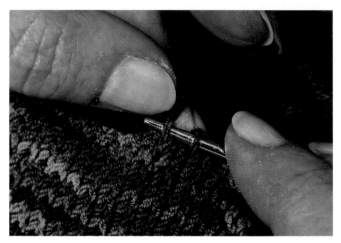

1. Pick up the live stitches from the invisible cast-on one at a time as you pull out each chain stitch and place them on the needle. Repeat this the length of the waist, picking up a total of 198 stitches.

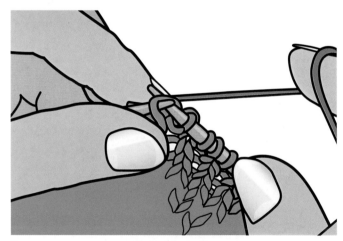

2. Place a marker. Knit the next stitch, then create a new stitch by knitting into the stitch below, lifting it first with your left-hand needle, then transferring it onto the right needle as you knit it. You should have 297 (324, 351) stitches on your needle when finished with this round.

3. If you are working the smallest or largest size, knit one round, increasing 1 stitch somewhere in the middle of the waist.

4. Knit 1 stitch, then slip the next stitch, holding the yarn in the front of the needle as you do so.

5. Return the yarn to its normal position and knit the next stitch.

6. Repeat Steps 4 and 5 the entire way around the waist.

7. When finished with Round 1, keep this skein of yarn at the front of the skirt as you begin Round 2.

8. Join the second skein of yarn and slip the first stitch, holding the yarn in back of the needle as you do so.

9. Return the yarn to its normal position, then purl 1 stitch.

10. Repeat Steps 8 and 9 the entire way around the waist. Leave this skein of yarn in the back as you work Round 1 for a second time.

11. Work these two rows 5 more times.

12. Place every other stitch on a spare circular needle, the same size or smaller.

Once every other stitch is separated onto two needles, the pocket created for the elastic becomes evident.

15. Using Kitchener stitch (see page 20), graft the stitches on the front and back needles together to close the casing at the top.

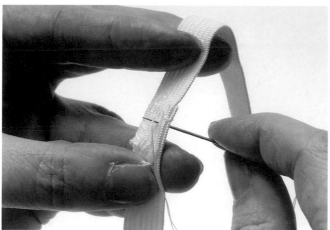

13. Whip stitch the ends of the elastic together using a needle and thread. Be sure to also whip stitch the edges together and along the back.

A dozen or so stitches grafted together to create the beginning of the casing

14. Place the elastic inside the pocket created by the two sides of the casing.

3

Twin Lakes Cover-up and Hat

Gauge: 19 sts and 20 rows to 4" in pattern on US 7 needle (or size to obtain gauge)

NOTE: To knit gauge swatch in pattern, CO 25 sts. K2 on each side of 21-stitch pattern. Measure for 19 sts.

Materials:

Medium weight Cotton/Rayon Blend, 200 yards/skein 2 (2, 3) skeins

US 7 Needle

Sample 1 knit in Rubble (78% Cotton, 20% Rayon, 2% Nylon) Color: Squirt

Sample 2 knit in Rubble (78% Cotton, 20% Rayon, 2% Nylon) Color: Natural

This adorable child's garment is the perfect choice for days at the beach or pool. Knit from a cotton/rayon blend in an open lacy pattern, the top and hat provide just the right balance of coverage and coolness to be worn over a bathing suit on hot summer days. This project introduces two useful skills: how to place shaping in a lace pattern and add ruffles to a garment. Following completion of the cover-up, moving on to the matching hat will also illustrate how a pattern knit in the flat can be adapted to knitting in the round.

COVER-UP

Measurements:
Finished Chest: 24 (26.5, 29)"
Finished Length: 17.5 (19, 21)"

BACK

CO 171 (189, 207) sts. K1 row.

Tip: Using stitch markers can help you keep track of lengthy cast-ons. Place markers after each 50 or 75 stitches.

RUFFLE

Row 1: Knit
Row 2, 4, 6, 8: k1, purl to last st, k1.
Row 3: [k1, k2tog] to end—114 (126, 138) sts.
Row 5: Knit.
Row 7: [k2tog] to end—57 (63, 69) sts.
Work 4 rows gar st.
Work in patt (below) with 3 gar st edge sts each side until piece measures 16.5 (18, 20)".

Tip: Don't just jump into the pattern—remember to knit the three edge stitches first.

PATTERN

Row 1 (RS), 3, 5, 7: * yo, sl1, k2tog, psso, yo, k3; rep from * to last 3 sts, yo, sl1, k2tog, psso, yo.
Row 2 and all even rows: Purl.
Row 9, 11, 13, 15: * k3, yo, sl1, k2tog, psso, yo; rep from * to last 3 sts, k3.
These 16 rows form pattern.

Tip: Measure frequently. As you get close to 16.5 (18, 20)", it's okay to stop in the middle of the pattern. Just make sure to use a row counter so you can pick up where you left off.

NECK SHAPING

Keeping continuity of patt, work 21 (23, 25) sts, place next 15 (17, 19) sts on hold, add another ball of yarn, work last 21 (23, 25) sts. BO 2 sts each neck edge 1x—19 (21, 23) sts. Work until piece measures 17.5 (19, 21)". Place shoulder sts on hold.

Tip: You can bind off the two neck-edge stitches on the wrong side in purl as you work your way back across, but you need to make sure to keep the tension on the first stitch from the new ball of yarn taut by pulling down on the newly added yarn. Bind off the two neck-edge stitches on the right side of the garment in knit.

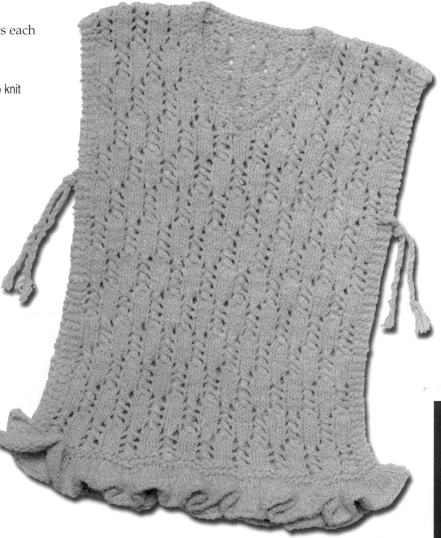

FRONT

Work as for back until piece measures 13.5 (14, 15.5)" (end with a WS row) then do neck shaping below.

NECK SHAPING

On a RS row, work 28 (31, 34) sts, place 1 st on hold, add another ball of yarn, work 28 (31, 34) sts.

Tip: Adding another ball of yarn can be tricky. It is sometimes easiest to move the balls of yarn from one side of your lap to the other as you turn the knitting from front to back.

Cont in patt, dec 1 st each neck edge every other row 6 (7, 8)x—22 (24, 26) sts each side. Dec 1 st each neck edge every fourth row 3x—19 (21, 23) sts. Work until piece measures 17.5 (19, 21)".

Make sure your decreases slant to the same side as the neckline: use a right-slanting decrease on the right side of the garment (see page 14) and a left-slanting decrease on the left side (see page 15).

When placing the decrease one stitch in from the edge of the row, always knit the stitch after the decrease (on the left side) or before the decrease (on the right side). Always count stitches at the end of each side to make sure you have the proper number of stitches. See the Skill Workshop on page 44 for further guidance on how to place these neck decreases.

FINISHING

Knit shoulder seams together with the three-needle bind off (see page 17 for a refresher on knitting shoulder seams together).

NECK BINDING

PU and knit 24 (26, 28) sts from left shoulder seam to center st, knit st on hold, PU and knit 24 (26, 28) sts to shoulder seam, PU and knit 4 sts to back holder, knit 15 (17, 19) sts from back holder, PU and knit 4 sts to shoulder seam. PM.

    Rnd 1: Purl.

    Rnd 2: Knit to within 2 sts of center marked st, ssk, k1, k2tog, knit to end.

    Rnd 3: Purl.

    BO loosely in knit.

TWIST TIE CLOSURE

Make twist tie for closure using a pencil or fringe twister. Weave tie through yo in lace to close.

Tip: See the Project in Progress on pages 48–50 for instructions on fringe twisting.

TIP

Make a hand-written chart of which rows you will need to do decreases and the corresponding number of total stitches you should have in that row. Use your row counter to keep track of where you are in the pattern. Cross off each decrease row as you complete it.
Always make decreases on odd-numbered rows. In this case it makes it easier to see the pattern in the lace.

Note: The example chart is for the smallest size.

(1), 2, (3), 4, (5), 6, (7), 8, (9), 10, (11) = 22 sts each side

12, 13, 14, (15), 16, 17, 18, (19), 20, 21, 22, (23), 24 = 19 sts each side

HAT

Measurements:

Finished Head Circumference: 16.5 (17.5, 19)"

Tip: Make a hat 1½" smaller than actual head circumference.

CO 243 (261, 279) sts. PM and join. P1 rnd.

Tip: It may work best to use three different needles to work this hat. Start out with a 24" circular, then change to a 16" circular, and finally to double points.

RUFFLE

Rnd 1: Knit.
Rnd 2: Knit.
Rnd 3: [k1, k2tog] to end—162 (174, 186) sts.
Rnd 4: Knit.
Rnd 5: Knit.
Rnd 6: Knit.
Rnd 7: [k2tog] to end—81 (87, 93) sts.
Rnd 8: Knit.
Rnd 9: Knit.
Rnd 10: Purl.
Rnd 11: Knit, dec 3 sts evenly around—78 (84, 90) sts.
Rnd 12: Purl.
Work Rnds 1 through 8 of patt.

Note: Work patt between *'s only because you are in the round. Work all WS rounds in knit.

Garter Ridge 1

Rnd 1: Knit dec 6 sts evenly around—72 (78, 84) sts.
Rnd 2: Purl.
Work Rnds 9 through 14 (16, 16) of patt.

Garter Ridge 2

Rnd 1: [k2tog] around—36 (39, 42) sts.
Rnd 2: Purl, dec 3 sts evenly around on 17.5" size only—36 (36, 42) sts.
Work Rnds 1 through 4 (6, 8) of patt.

FINISHING

Rnd 1: [k2tog] around—18 (18, 21) sts.
Rnd 2: Purl.
Rnd 3: Knit dec 6 sts evenly around—12 (12, 15) sts.
Rnd 4: Knit.
Rnd 5: Same as Rnd 3—6 (6, 9) sts.
Rnd 6: Knit.
Cut yarn leaving an 8" tail. Thread tail using a tapestry needle. Work tapestry needle through each live st as you remove them from knitting needles. Draw tight and fasten off.

When working in a lace pattern with yarn overs, decreases—such as at the neck edge—can be tricky. This Skill Workshop will show how to achieve the decreases in the neck shaping while still managing to maintain the lace pattern. It may help to think of decreasing as eliminating stitches from the lace pattern from the right edge. As you eliminate these edges you still need to maintain the vertical integrity of the lace pattern.

1. Cast on 20 stitches and work 4 rows of stockinette to start your swatch. Work the first 6 rows of the lace pattern for this garment, but with a knit stitch at each edge:

Row 1 (RS): k1 (edge stitch), * yo, sl1, k2tog, psso, yo, k3; rep from * to last stitch, knit (edge stitch).

Row 2 and all even rows: Purl.

2. Knit the edge stitch on the swatch.

3. To make the decrease, omit the yarn over from the pattern, and continue by slipping the next stitch.

4. Then knit the next 2 stitches together and pass the slipped stitch over, as in the pattern.

5. Now work the yarn over and continue with the row as printed. The finished row will have 19 stitches.

6. Purl Row 2 (wrong side). Then on the next right-side row, you will decrease again. You have now eliminated the edge stitch, so you will start by slipping the first stitch in the row.

7. Knit the next 2 stitches together and pass the slipped stitch over.

8. Work the yarn over and continue with the row as printed. The finished row will have 18 stitches.

9. Purl the next row (wrong side). Then on the next right-side row, you will decrease again. You have eliminated the first lace section, so in order to maintain the integrity of the pattern, you need to work your decrease before reaching the knit 3 section: Slip the first stitch in the row, knit the next stitch and pass the slipped stitch over this single knit stitch.

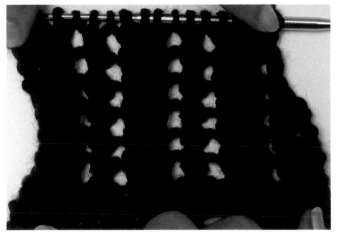

10. Continue with the pattern (knit 3), then work the next lace section as the pattern indicates. The finished row will have 17 stitches.

To continue decreasing, continue eliminating stitches from the right-hand edge one at a time, always working to maintain the vertical integrity of the lace pattern.

Ruffles are easy to make and can be tailored to fit the length of any garment's edge. Simply multiply the final desired stitches by 3; this gives you the number of stitches to cast on. For example, in this hat, you cast on 243 (261, 279) stitches to create a ruffle that matches a finished edge of 81 (87, 93) stitches (after round 7).

You can control the degree to which the ruffle curls by adjusting the groupings of stitches in the decreases. See how this works by creating two swatches.

Cast on 20 stitches and work a 4-row garter stitch border. To create a gently curling ruffle, follow this pattern:

3. Purl the wrong-side row. On the right-side row, * knit 1, then knit 2 together. Repeat from *. The finished row will have 8 stitches.

1. Row 1 (RS), * knit 3 then knit 2 together. Repeat from *. The finished row will have 16 stitches.

4. Purl the wrong-side row. On the right-side row, * knit 2 together. Repeat from *.

2. Purl the wrong-side row. On the right-side row, * knit 2, then knit 2 together. Repeat from *. The finished row will have 12 stitches.

5. The finished row will have 4 stitches.

Twin Lakes Cover-up and Hat

To make a more quickly curling ruffle, you need to work decreases only, with no knit stitches in between. Cast on 20 stitches and work a 4-row garter stitch border.

1. Row 1 (RS): * knit 2 together. Repeat from *. The finished row will have 10 stitches.

2. Purl the wrong-side row. On the right-side row, * knit 2 together. Repeat from *.

3. The finished row will have 5 stitches.

Compare the two finished ruffles:

The gently curling ruffle

The more quickly curling ruffle

You can also shorten or lengthen a ruffle by adjusting the number of knit and purl rows between the decrease rows. For a shorter ruffle, include fewer rows between the decreases; for a longer ruffle, add more.

47

Making the Twist Tie Closure

Since this is a bathing suit cover-up, you don't want to sew the side seams together, but it is important to connect them well enough that the garment isn't flapping in the wind. The solution: a simple twist tie closure. You can purchase a commercially available fringe twister to do the job for you (see the Resources page for a supplier suggestion), or you can create your own fringe using a pencil to twist the two groups of yarn. You may need to practice a few times before you get the cord to look just right.

1. Cut two 36-inch lengths of the project yarn.

3. Hold the knotted lengths of yarn in your left hand and with your right hand insert the pencil between the two of the strands of yarn at the very top, just below the knot.

4. Pinch the yarn tightly between your left thumb and index finger, just below the pencil.

2. Hold the strands parallel and tie knots at both ends.

Twin Lakes Cover-up and Hat

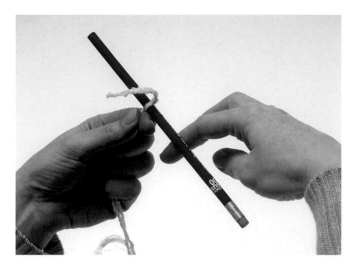

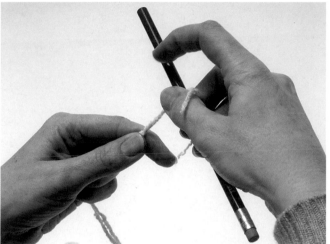

5. With your right hand, slowly twist the pencil in a clockwise motion, continuing to pinch the yarn gently between your thumb and index finger.

7. When you reach the end of the yarn, bring the knotted ends together at the pencil end. The cord should twist up on its own.

6. Gently pull down on the yarn as you go, continuing to twist with the pencil. Don't overtwist; make sure to keep pulling down at a fairly steady pace.

8. Slip the end of the cord off the pencil and knot the two knotted ends together.

9. Tie a knot at the other end of the cord, about ¾"
down from the end.

The finished twist tie closure

10. Cut the end of the cord below the knot and loosen
the strands for fringe.

4

Lantz Corners Shawl

Gauge: Wet Blocked Gauge

15 sts and 21 rows to 4"
in St st on US 8 needle
(or size to obtain gauge)

Measurements: 40" x 40"

Materials:

DK weight Cotton Blend
(3) 200 yards/skein,
5 skeins

US 8 Double Pointed
Needles (or size to obtain
gauge)

US 8 16" Circular Needle
(or size to obtain gauge)

US 8 24" Circular Needle
(or size to obtain gauge)

NOTE: Some knitters may prefer
a circular needle longer
than 24" when working
with all stitches to avoid
overcrowding of stitches
on the needle. Consider
opting for a 36" circular,
if available.

Sample knit in Dunluce
(57% Cotton, 38% Rayon,
5% Linen) Color: Natural

This intricate design starts in the center
and works outward, building from just
eight cast-on stitches to a final round con-
taining 520 stitches. Its airy beauty is created
by a complex lace pattern knit in the round
and then bound off using a special technique
that allows for abundant elasticity. The cotton
blend chosen for the project gives the piece
a lightness and flexibility that accentuates the
open pattern of the lace. When complete, the
square piece can be folded in half, triangle-
style, and worn as a shawl or used as a
square for a small table cover.

SHAWL

CO 8 sts. Divide sts evenly onto 4 double pointed needles with 2 sts on each needle. PM, join, and knit 1 rnd.

Note: From this point forward all instructions will be repeated around. Each instruction will be worked a total of 4x around. To calculate number of sts in a rnd, multiply the st number at the end of each instruction by 4. (See the Project in Progress on pages 55–57 for a further explanation.)

Rnd 1: yo, k1, yo, k1—4 sts.

Rnd 2 (and all other even rounds unless otherwise specified): Knit.

Rnd 3: yo, k1, yo, ssk, yo, k1—6 sts.

Rnd 5: yo, k2tog, yo, k1, yo, ssk, yo, k1—8 sts.

Rnd 7: yo, k2, yo, p3tog, yo, k2, yo, k1—10 sts.

Rnd 9: yo, k1, k2tog, yo, k3, yo, ssk, k1, yo, k1—12 sts.

Rnd 11: yo, k3, yo, k1, p3tog, k1, yo, k3, yo, k1—14 sts.

Rnd 13: yo, k2, k2tog, yo, k5, yo, ssk, k2, yo, k1—16 sts.

Rnd 15: yo, k4, yo, k2, p3tog, k2, yo, k4, yo, k1—18 sts.

Rnd 17: yo, k3, k2tog, yo, k7, yo, ssk, k3, yo, k1—20 sts.

Rnd 19: yo, k5, yo, k3, p3tog, k3, yo, k5, yo, k1—22 sts.

Rnd 21: yo, k4, k2tog, yo, k9, yo, ssk, k4, yo, k1—24 sts.

Rnd 23: yo, k6, yo, k4, p3tog, k4, yo, k6, yo, k1—26 sts.

Rnd 25: yo, k5, k2tog, yo, k11, yo, ssk, k5, yo, k1—28 sts.

Rnd 27: yo, k7, yo, k5, p3tog, k5, yo, k7, yo, k1—30 sts.

Rnd 29: yo, k6, k2tog, yo, k1, yo, ssk, k7, k2tog, yo, k1, yo, ssk, k6, yo, k1—32 sts.

Rnd 31: yo, k8, yo, p3tog, yo, k9, yo, p3tog, yo, k8, yo, k1—34 sts.

Rnd 33: yo, k7, k2tog, yo, k3, yo, ssk, k5, k2tog, yo, k3, yo, ssk, k7, yo, k1—36 sts.

Rnd 35: yo, k9, yo, k1, p3tog, k1, yo, k7, yo, k1, p3tog, k1, yo, k9, yo, k1—38 sts.

Rnd 37: yo, k8, k2tog, yo, k5, yo, ssk, k3, k2tog, yo, k5, yo, ssk, k8, yo, k1—40 sts.

Rnd 39: yo, k10, yo, k2, p3tog, k2, yo, k5, yo, k2, p3tog, k2, yo, k10, yo, k1—42 sts.

Rnd 41: yo, k9, k2tog, yo, k7, yo, ssk, k1, k2tog, yo, k7, yo, ssk, k9, yo, k1—44 sts.

Rnd 43: yo, k11, yo, k3, p3tog, k3, yo, k3, yo, k3, p3tog, k3, yo, k11, yo, k1—46 sts.

Rnd 45: yo, k10, k2tog, yo, k9, yo, sl1, k2tog, psso, yo, k9, yo, ssk, k10, yo, k1—48 sts.

Rnd 47: yo, k10, k2tog, yo, k4, p3tog, k4, yo [k1, yo, k1] into next st, yo, k4, p3tog, k4, yo, ssk, k10, yo, k1—50 sts.

Rnd 49: yo, k10, k2tog, yo, k11, yo, sl1, k2tog, psso, yo, k11, yo, ssk, k10, yo, k1—52 sts.

Rnd 51: yo, k12, yo, k5, p3tog, k5, yo, k1, yo, k5, p3tog, k5, yo, k12, yo, k1—54 sts.

Rnd 53: yo, k11, k2tog, yo, ssk, k9, k2tog, yo [k1, yo, k1] into next st, yo, ssk, k9, k2tog, yo, ssk, k11, yo, k1—56 sts.

Rnd 55: yo, k11, k2tog, yo, k1, yo, ssk, k7, k2tog, yo, k2tog, yo, k1, yo, k2tog, yo, ssk, k7, k2tog, yo, k1, yo, ssk, k11, yo, k1—58 sts.

Rnd 57: yo, k9 [k2tog] 2x, yo, k1 [k1, yo, k1] into next st, k1, yo, ssk, k5, k2tog, yo, k1, ssk, k1, k2tog, k1, yo, ssk, k5, k2tog, yo, k1 [k1, yo, k1] into next st, k1, yo [ssk] 2x, k9, yo, k1—60 sts.

Rnd 59: yo, k10, k2tog, yo, k2tog, yo, k3, yo, k2tog, yo [ssk, k3, k2tog, yo, k2tog, yo, k3, yo, ssk, yo] 2x, ssk, k10, yo, k1—62 sts.

Rnd 61: yo, k8 [k2tog] 2x [yo, k2tog] 2x, yo, k1 [yo, k2tog] 2x, yo, ssk, k1, k2tog, yo, k2tog, yo, k2, yo, k1, yo, k2, yo, k2tog, yo, ssk, k1, k2tog [yo, k2tog] 2x, yo, k1 [yo, k2tog] 2x, yo [ssk] 2x, k8, yo, k1—64 sts.

Rnd 63: yo, k9, k2tog, yo [k2tog, yo] 2x, k3 [yo, k2tog] 2x, yo, sl1, k2tog, psso, yo [k2tog, yo] 3x, k1 [yo, k2tog] 3x, yo, sl1, k2tog, psso, yo [k2tog, yo] 2x, k3 [yo, k2tog] 2x, yo, ssk, k9, yo, k1—66 sts.

Rnd 65: yo, k7 [k2tog] 2x, yo [k2tog, yo] 3x, k1 [yo, ssk] 3x, yo, k1, yo [k2tog, yo] 3x, sl1, k2tog, psso [yo, ssk] 3x, yo, k1, yo [k2tog, yo] 3x, k1 [yo, ssk] 3x, yo [ssk] 2x, k7, yo, k1—68 sts.

Rnd 67: yo, k8, k2tog, yo [k2tog, yo] 3x, k3 [yo, ssk] 3x, k1 [k2tog, yo] 3x, k3 [yo, ssk] 3x, k1 [k2tog, yo] 3x, k3 [yo, ssk] 3x, yo, ssk, k8, yo, k1—70 sts.

Rnd 69: yo, k6 [k2tog] 2x, yo [k2tog, yo] 4x, k1 [yo, ssk] 3x, k3 [k2tog, yo] 2x, k1, yo, k3, yo, k1 [yo, ssk] 2x, k3 [k2tog, yo] 3x, k1 [yo, ssk] 4x, yo [ssk] 2x, k6, yo, k1—72 sts.

Rnd 71: yo, k7, k2tog, yo [k2tog, yo] 4x, k3 [yo, ssk] 3x, k1 [k2tog, yo] 4x, k1 [yo, ssk] 4x, k1 [k2tog, yo] 3x, k3 [yo, ssk] 4x, yo, ssk, k7, yo, k1—74 sts.

Rnd 73: yo, k5 [k2tog] 2x, yo [k2tog, yo] 5x, k1 [yo, ssk] 3x, yo, k3, yo [k2tog, yo] 2x, k2tog, k3, ssk [yo, ssk] 2x, yo, k3, yo [k2tog, yo] 3x, k1 [yo, ssk] 5x, yo [ssk] 2x, k5, yo, k1—76 sts.

Rnd 75: yo, k6, k2tog, yo [k2tog, yo] 5x, k3 [yo, ssk] 3x, yo, sl1, k2tog, psso, yo [k2tog, yo] 3x, k3 [yo, ssk] 3x, yo, k3tog, yo [k2tog, yo] 3x, k3 [yo, ssk] 5x, yo, ssk, k6, yo, k1—78 sts.

Rnd 77: yo, k4 [k2tog] 2x, yo [k2tog, yo] 6x, k1 [yo, ssk] 5x, k1, yo [k2tog, yo] 3x, k1 [yo, ssk] 3x, k1, yo [k2tog, yo] 5x, k1 [yo, ssk] 6x, yo [ssk] 2x, k4, yo, k1—80 sts.

Rnd 79: yo, k5, k2tog, yo [k2tog, yo] 6x, k3 [yo, ssk] 5x [k2tog, yo] 3x, k3 [yo, ssk] 3x [k2tog, yo] 5x, k3 [yo, ssk] 6x, yo, ssk, k5, yo, k1—82 sts.

Rnd 81: yo, k3 [k2tog] 2x, yo [k2tog, yo] 7x, k1 [yo, ssk] 6x, yo [k2tog, yo] 3x, k1 [yo, ssk] 3x, yo [k2tog, yo] 6x, k1 [yo, ssk] 7x, yo [ssk] 2x, k3, yo, k1—84 sts.

Rnd 83: yo, k4, k2tog, yo [k2tog, yo] 7x, k3 [yo, ssk] 5x, yo, sl1, k2tog, psso, yo [k2tog, yo] 2x, k3 [yo, ssk] 2x, yo, k3tog, yo [k2tog, yo] 5x, k3 [yo, ssk] 7x, yo, ssk, k4, yo, k1—86 sts.

Rnd 85: yo, k2 [k2tog] 2x, yo [k2tog, yo] 8x, k1 [yo, ssk] 7x, k1, yo [k2tog, yo] 2x, k1 [yo, ssk] 2x, yo, k1 [k2tog, yo] 7x, k1 [yo, ssk] 8x, yo [ssk] 2x, k2, yo, k1—88 sts.

Rnd 87: yo, k3, k2tog, yo [k2tog, yo] 8x, k3 [yo, ssk] 7x [k2tog, yo] 2x, k3 [yo, ssk] 2x [k2tog, yo] 7x, k3 [yo, ssk] 8x, yo, ssk, k3, yo, k1—90 sts.

Rnd 89: yo, k1 [k2tog] 2x, yo [k2tog, yo] 9x, k1 [yo, ssk] 8x, yo [k2tog, yo] 2x, k1 [yo, ssk] 2x, yo [k2tog, yo] 8x, k1 [yo, ssk] 9x, yo [ssk] 2x, k1, yo, k1—92 sts.

Rnd 91: yo, k2, k2tog, yo [k2tog, yo] 9x, k3 [yo, ssk] 8x, k1, k2tog, yo, k3, yo, ssk, k1 [k2tog, yo] 8x, k3 [yo, ssk] 9x, yo, ssk, k2, yo, k1—94 sts.

Rnd 93: yo [k2tog] 2x, yo [k2tog, yo] 10x, k1 [yo, ssk] 9x, k1, yo, k2tog, yo, k1, yo, ssk, yo, k1 [k2tog, yo] 9x, k1 [yo, ssk] 10x, yo [ssk] 2x, yo, k1—96 sts.

Rnd 95: yo, k1, k2tog, yo [k2tog, yo] 10x, k3 [yo, ssk] 9x, k2tog, yo, k3, yo, ssk [k2tog, yo] 9x, k3 [yo, ssk] 10x, yo, ssk, k1, yo, k1—98 sts.

Rnd 97: yo, k3tog, yo [k2tog, yo] 11x, k1 [yo, ssk] 10x, yo, k2tog, yo, k1, yo, ssk, yo [k2tog, yo] 10x, k1 [yo, ssk] 11x, yo, sl1, k2tog, psso, yo, k1—100 sts.

Rnd 99: yo [k2tog, yo] 12x, k3 [yo, ssk] 10x, k2tog, yo, k1, yo, ssk [k2tog, yo] 10x, k3 [yo, ssk] 12x, yo, k1—102 sts.

Rnd 101: yo, knit to last st, yo, k1—104 sts.

Rnd 102: k1, purl to last 2 sts, k2—104 sts.

Rnd 103: yo, k6, * k4, k2tog, yo, k1, yo, ssk, k4; rep from * to last 7 sts, k6, yo, k1—106 sts.

Rnd 105: yo, k2, yo, ssk, k3, * k3, k2tog, yo, k3, yo, ssk, k3; rep from * to last 8 sts, k3, k2tog, yo, k2, yo, k1—108 sts.

Rnd 107: yo, k2 [yo, ssk] 2x, k2, * k2 [k2tog, yo] 2x, k1 [yo, ssk] 2x, k2; rep from * to last 9 sts, k2 [k2tog, yo] 2x, k2, yo, k1—110 sts.

Rnd 109: yo, k4 [yo, ssk] 2x, k2, * k1 [k2tog, yo] 2x, k3 [yo, ssk] 2x, k2; rep from * to last 10 sts, k1 [k2tog, yo] 2x, k4, yo, k1—112 sts.

Rnd 111: yo, k1, k2tog, yo, k1 [yo, ssk] 3x, * [k2tog, yo] 3x, k1 [yo, ssk] 3x; rep from * to last 11 sts [k2tog, yo] 3x, k1, yo, ssk, k1, yo, k1—114 sts.

Rnd 113: as rnd 101—116 sts.

Rnd 114: as rnd 102—116 sts.

Rnd 115: yo, k1 [ssk, yo] 2x, k1 [yo, k2tog] 3x, * [ssk, yo] 3x, k1 [yo, k2tog] 3x; rep from * to last 13 sts [ssk, yo] 3x, k1 [yo, k2tog] 2x, k1, yo, k1—118 sts.

Rnd 117: yo, * k1 [ssk, yo] 2x, k3 [yo, k2tog] 2x, k1; rep from * to last st, yo, k1—120 sts.

Rnd 119: yo, k1, * k2 [ssk, yo] 2x, k1 [yo, k2tog] 2x, k2; rep from * to last 2 sts, k1, yo, k1—122 sts.

Rnd 121: yo, k2, * k3, ssk, yo, k3, yo, k2tog, k3; rep from * to last 3 sts, k2, yo, k1—124 sts.

Rnd 123: yo, k3, * k4, ssk, yo, k1, yo, k2tog, k4; rep from * to last 4 sts, k3, yo, k1—126 sts.

Rnd 125: as rnd 101—128 sts.

Rnd 126: as rnd 102—128 sts.

Rnd 127: as rnd 101—130 sts.

Rnd 128: as rnd 102—130 sts.

BO using twice-worked BO in purl, as follows: purl 2 sts, BO, * return st on right-hand needle to left-hand needle, p2tog, p1, BO; rep from * to end.

Note: See the Skill Workshop on pages 58–59 for more details on this bind-off technique.

Switching from Double Pointed to Circular Needles

One of the most interesting aspects of this project is how it "grows" from just 8 stitches to more than 500 before it is finished. Because there are so few stitches in the beginning, it is necessary to start the project on double pointed (DP) needles. As the DP needles get full, you will switch to your circular needle, knitting the stitches off the double points and onto the circular. This Project in Progress will walk you through the first 20 rows of the project and indicate the best point at which to make this transition.

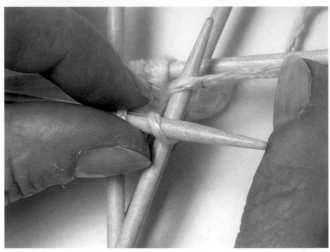

3. While still lying flat, join and knit one round.

1. Cast on 8 stitches and divide evenly between four DP needles.

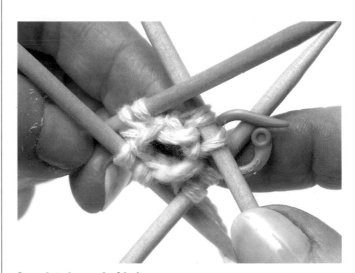

Completed round of knit

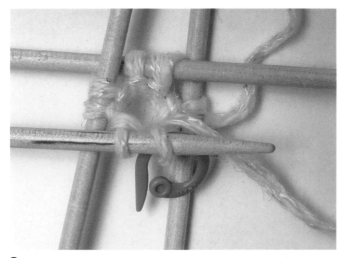

2. Lay the needles flat in a square shape and place a split marker on the first stitch.

Tip: Knitting with four double pointed needles with so few stitches is unwieldy at first. Proper tension is essential to help keep the needles in place. Be patient, work slowly, and know that it will get easier as you add more stitches to the needles.

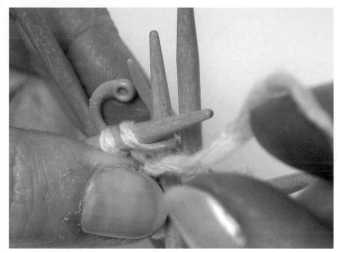

4. To start Round 1, do a yarn over first, holding it to the needle as you knit the next stitch.

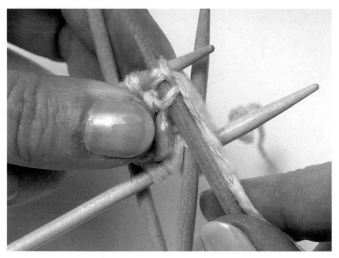

5. Knit the next stitch.

6. Do another yarn over and knit 1 to put 4 stitches on this needle. Repeat the yo, k1, yo, k1 on the remaining three needles until there are 16 stitches total.

Note: Starting in Round 1, the instruction is only printed once, but it is intended to be applied to the entire round (four times total). To figure out the total number of stitches you should have at the end of each round, multiply the number of stitches listed at the end of each instruction by four. So in Round 1, for example, you should have 16 stitches on your needles at the end of this round. By the time you reach Round 128, you will have a total of 520 (4 x 130) stitches on your needles.

7. Knit Round 2. All even rows are knit unless specified otherwise.

8. Knit Round 3: yo, k1, yo, ssk, yo, k1. Repeat on the other three needles. You will have 24 stitches on the needles at the end of this round.

Tip: You'll notice that it's relatively easy to make sure you have the right number of stitches while you're knitting on the DP needles; because you've divided the stitches between four needles, each needle should have the number of stitches listed at the end of the round.

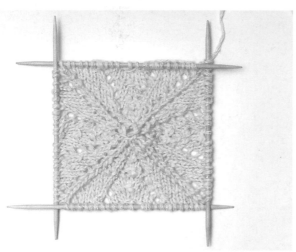

9. Continue in the pattern through Round 19, at which point you should have a total of 22 stitches on each DP needle (a total of 88 stitches in the round).

The marker at the beginning of the round was blue; use a different color marker at the beginning of each needle so you can tell where the round begins.

10. Before starting Round 20, switch to your circular needle. As you knit stitches off each DP needle onto the circular needle, place a marker at the beginning of the first stitch from each needle. This will help you ensure that the total number of stitches per round is correct. The number at the end of each round should correspond with the number of stitches between each marker. Make sure to place a different-colored marker at the start of the round.

All 88 stitches transferred from the double pointed needles to the circular needle

Tip: A round counter is essential for this project, as it becomes difficult to keep track of where you are in the pattern. It may also be helpful to use a magnet board (available in many knitting and counted cross-stitch supply stores) to help keep your place in the printed pattern, or you could photocopy the pattern page from the book and highlight each row as you complete it.

SKILL WORKSHOP: TWICE-WORKED BIND OFF

This kind of project requires a special bind off in order to make sure that the edge does not pull or pucker. Master knitter Judy Pascale developed this special "twice-worked bind off" technique for use in her Shapely Shawlette patterns (see page 116 for details). It allows for abundant elasticity.

1. Cast on 20 stitches and work a 20-row swatch in stockinette. Then work 4 rows of a garter stitch border.

3. Return the stitch on the right-hand needle to the left-hand needle.

4. Purl these 2 stitches together.

2. Purl the first 2 stitches of the next round, then bind off the first stitch.

5. Now purl a second stitch.

The finished bound-off edge shows the elasticity that this bind-off method produces.

6. Bind off the first stitch on the needle.

7. Repeat from Step 3, and continue until all stitches are bound off.

5

Tracy Ridge Hat

Gauge: 40 sts/56 rows to 5" on US 4 needle or size to obtain gauge (see note below)

Measurements:

Finished Circumference: 20 (22)"

Materials:

Fingering weight yarn, 200 yards/sk, 2 skeins [1]

US 3 and 4, 16" Circular Needles

Toggle (sample uses La Mode 4799)

Sample 1 knit in Cherub (100% Merino Wool) Color: Natural

Sample 2 knit in Cherub Colors: Cotton Candy (MC), Parrot (CC), 1 skein each

NOTE: Gauge swatch is worked over 44 sts, set up as follows: 2 edge sts, 12 sts patt 1, 28 sts patt 2, 2 edge sts. Measure only 40 sts and 56 rows of swatch

Cables and bobbles make this hat an instant classic, whether you choose to knit it in a more traditional solid neutral hue or in more vibrant contrasting colors. The interesting texture in the hat is achieved through alternating two separate patterns within each round. The hat is worked from the bottom up and the drawstring closure makes this a quick knit. Although modeled here by a woman, this hat would be an equally stylish accessory for a man.

Note: Since the pattern is designed to be knit in the round and your gauge swatch will be knit flat, it is necessary to simulate round knitting by carrying the yarn across the back of the swatch rather than turning the swatch and knitting a wrong and right side.

The wrong side of the gauge swatch

PATTERN I

Rnd 1 (RS): Purl.

Rnd 2: * (p1, k1, p1) into next st, k3tog; rep from * to end.

Rnd 3: Purl.

Rnd 4: * k3tog, (p1, k1, p1) into next st; rep from * to end.

PATTERN II

Rnd 1 (RS): * P4, k1, p1, k4, p1, k1; rep from * to last 4 sts, p4.

Rnd 2: * p4, k1, p1, k4, p1, k1; rep from * to last 4 sts, p4.

Rnd 3: * p4, k1, p1, C4F, p1, k1; rep from * to last 4 sts, p4.

Rnd 4: * p4, k1, p1, k4, p1, k1; rep from * to last 4 sts, p4.

Rnd 5: * p4, k1, p1, k4, p1, k1; rep from * to last 4 sts, p4.

Rnd 6: * p4, k1, p1, k4, p1, k1; rep from * to last 4 sts, p4.

Rnd 7: * p4, k1, p1, C4F, p1, k1; rep from * to last 4 sts, p4.

Rnd 8: * p4, k1, p1, k4, p1, k1; rep from * to last 4 sts, p4.

Rnd 9: * p4, k1, p1, k4, p1, k1; rep from * to last 4 sts, p4.

Rnd 10: * p4, k1, p1, k4, p1, k1; rep from * to last 4 sts, p4.

Rnd 11: * p4, k1, p1, C4F, p1, k1; rep from * to last 4 sts, p4.

Rnd 12: * p4, k1, p1, k4, p1, k1; rep from * to last 4 sts, p4.

Rnd 13: * p4, k8; rep from * to last 4 sts, p4.

Rnd 14: * p4, k8; rep from * to last 4 sts, p4.

Rnd 15: * p4, k8; rep from * to last 4 sts, p4.

Rnd 16: * p4, k8; rep from * to last 4 sts, p4.

Rnd 17: * p4, C8F; rep from * to last 4 sts, p4.

Rnd 18: * p4, k8; rep from * to last 4 sts, p4.

Rnd 19: * p4, k8; rep from * to last 4 sts, p4.

Rnd 20: * p4, k8; rep from * to last 4 sts, p4.

C4F: Place 2 stitches on cable needle, hold at front of work, knit 2 stitches from left-hand needle, knit 2 stitches from cable needle.

Tip: The rule of thumb is to make your hat 1½" smaller than actual head circumference.

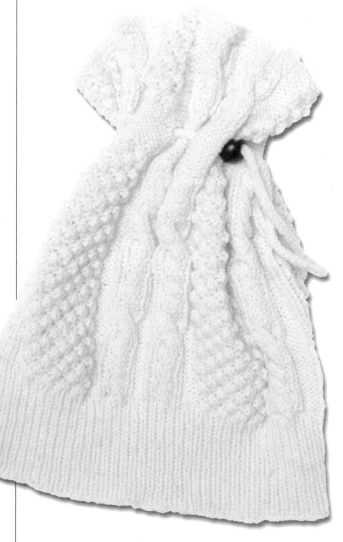

C8F: Place 4 stitches on cable needle, hold at front of work, knit 4 stitches from left-hand needle, knit 4 stitches from cable needle.

HAT

With smaller needle, CO 150 (160) sts. PM and join. Work 1 x 1 ribbing until piece measures 2.5" inc 10 (16) sts evenly on last round—160 (176) sts.

TIPS

- Place markers after each set of 40 (44) stitches to help keep track of the pattern. Make sure the marker at the beginning of the round is a different color.
- If knitting in two colors, knit one round in MC before switching to CC.

With larger needle, set up patt as follows: * work 12 (16) sts patt I, work 28 sts patt II; rep from * around. Continue working rows of each patt as established until you have completed 2 sets patt II and an additional 12 rnds of patt II.

Dec Rnd: * [p2, p2tog] 3x (4x), p4, [p2tog, p4] 4x; rep from * around—132 (144) sts.

P4 rnds.

Eyelet Rnd: * p10, yo, p2tog; rep from * around.

P4 rnds.

Inc Rnd: * [p2, inc in next st] 3x (4x), p4 [inc in next st, p4] 4x; rep from * around—160 (176) sts.

Set up patt as previously worked beg with Rnd 9 of patt II and ending with Rnd 4 of patt II for a total of 16 rnds.

Dec Rnd: * [k2, k2tog] 3x (4x), k4 [k2tog, k4] 4x; rep from * around—132 (144).

P1 row.

K1 row.

P1 row.

BO.

TIE

With smaller needle, work 3 st I-cord† as follows: CO 3 sts, * k3, push sts to other end of needle, k3; rep from * until tie measures 12". Do not bind off. Weave free end of cord through eyelets of hat. Weave 3 live sts of I-cord to cast on edge of I-cord joining into a circle. (See steps 8–15 of the Project in Progress on pages 77–78 for instructions on how to do this.) Place cord through ends of toggle and tighten.

OPTIONAL: Work hat in 2 colors.

MC—Cotton Candy

CC—Parrot

Use MC for patt I, patt II, I-cord.

Use CC for ribbing, rev St st, gar st.

Note: Between all changes of color, the knitter must work 1 rnd of knit. This will ensure that no odd colors of yarn will pop up with a purl stitch.

† I-cord is a name first coined by knitting pioneer Elizabeth Zimmerman to describe easy-to-knit, decorative cording. See page 19 for a refresher on how to make I-cord.

Tracy Ridge Hat

Graphs provide a visual representation of the stitches in a repeat and give a better indication of how the finished motif will look. Although they may look overwhelming at first, once mastered, graphs offer an enhanced way to view a pattern.

The practice of representing stitches in graphic form is known as Symbolcraft. Different stitches are represented by different graphic symbols. Each symbol represents how the stitch will look on the right-hand side of the work. Each square of the graph equals one stitch. Each line of the graph equals one row of knitting.

For flat knitting, graphs are read from right to left on right-side rows and from left to right on wrong-side rows, and graphs are usually numbered as such. All graphs are read from bottom to top.

Below is an example of the Symbolcraft for this sample 10-stitch pattern (knit flat):

Row 1 (RS): p4, k1, p1, k4
Row 2: p3, k2, p2, k3
Row 3: p2, k2, p1, k1, p2, k2
Row 4: p1, k2, p2, k2, p2, k1
Row 5: k2, p3, k3, p2
Row 6: k1, p4, k4, p1

However, in circular knitting, the graph is always read from right to left. The graph below is for the 12-stitch repeat of Pattern I for the Tracy Ridge Hat:

Rnd 1 (RS): Purl.
Rnd 2: * (p1, k1, p1) into next st, k3tog; rep from * to end.
Rnd 3: Purl.
Rnd 4: * k3tog, (p1, k1, p1) into next st; rep from * to end.

Sample 10-stitch pattern

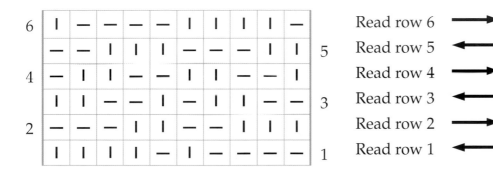

Pattern I—12 STS

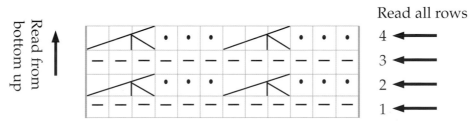

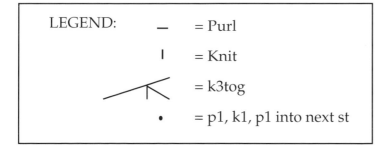

LEGEND:

    — = Purl

    I = Knit

    ⅄ = k3tog

    • = p1, k1, p1 into next st

NOTES:

In circular knitting, read all patterns R to L.

Read all patterns bottom to top.

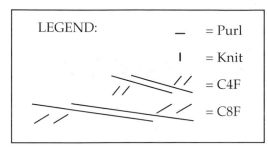

LEGEND:

— = Purl

I = Knit

= C4F

= C8F

NOTES:

In circular knitting, read all patterns R to L.

Read all patterns bottom to top.

Tracy Ridge Hat

Read all rows ⟵

Pattern II—28 STS

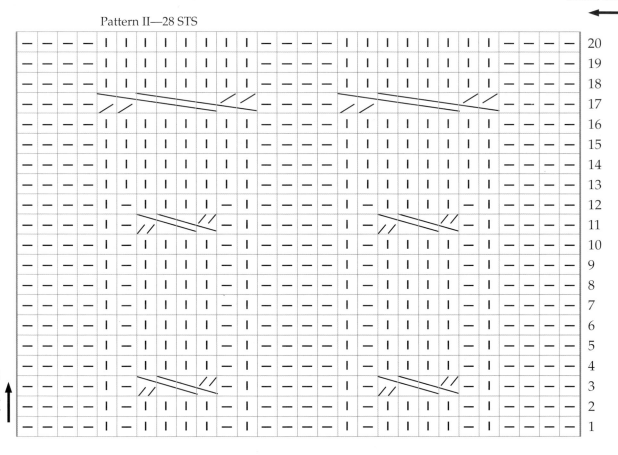

Read from bottom up

More complex patterns are represented in the same way, just on a larger scale. Graphs of larger patterns also make it easier to see the texture of a repeated motif. The graph of Pattern II of the Tracy Ridge Hat, for example, provides a very good graphic representation of the cabled motif as it recurs throughout the pattern.

Some knitters prefer reading graphs to written instructions. Some patterns provide both graphs and written instructions for those who prefer one method over another. The ability to read both will prepare you to work with whatever representation the pattern-maker chooses.

6

Beaver Meadows Felted Purse

Gauge: 12 sts and 14 rows to 4" in St st on US 11 needles (or size to obtain gauge)

Measurements: Finished bottom rectangle: 9" x 5"

Height: 8"

Materials:

Worsted weight wool (4) (100% wool, 200 yds/skein), 1 skein green (A), 1 skein blue (B)

Fingering weight 100% Merino Yarn (1) (200 yds/skein) 1 skein each: green (C), light pink (D), blue (E), red (F)

US 11 24" Circular Needle (or size to obtain gauge)

US 8 Double Pointed Needles (or size to obtain gauge)

Size K Crochet Hook

Tapestry Needle

6 large yellow buttons flower centers (JHB #53291 used in sample)

9" x 5" piece of plastic for bottom of bag

NOTE: All yarns used in this project must be 100% wool in order to felt properly.

Samples knit in Star City Wool (100% Wool): Green (A), Blue (B)

Cherub (100% Merino Wool): Parrot (C), Cotton Candy (D), Raspberry Fizz (E), Red Red Wine (F)

Felted bags have become increasingly popular in recent years, and with good reason. Knit loosely on large needles and then shrunk down through washing in hot water, these projects can be completed in much less time than it would appear. The floral appliqué work in this project adds an element of whimsy to the traditional felted purse. The Project in Progress section beginning on page 71 walks you through creating and attaching the appliqué, which is done prior to the felting process. Creating the mitred rectangle that forms the base of the purse also introduces a useful skill and provides ample practice with left- and right-slanting decreases.

RECTANGULAR BOTTOM

Tip: See the Project in Progress on page 68 for practice with creating a mitred rectangle before starting this project.

With A, CO 128 sts on circular needle. Mark 1st, 20th, 65th, 84th cast-on sts. 1st marked st signifies beginning of round. Hold needles with 1st cast-on st in left hand and last cast-on st in right hand.

Rnd 1 (dec rnd): To join rnd, slip last cast-on from right needle to left needle, * sl 2 sts tog as if to knit, k1,

p2sso, knit to within 1 st of next marked corner, rep from * 2x more, sl 2 sts tog as if to knit, k1, p2sso, knit to 1st marked st.

Tip: Even with the marker at the bottom of the row, you should easily be able to follow the marked stitch by the stockinette ridge created by the decreases.

Rnd 2: * k1, purl to next marked st, rep from * 2x more, k1, purl to within 1 st of 1st marked st.

Repeat these last 2 rnds until mitred corners meet. Complete this row, then k1 st more so sts can be divided evenly. Place 1st 28 sts on spare needle. With right side facing, BO 28 sts using 3 needle BO.

Tip: See page 17 for a refresher on the three-needle bind off.

SIDES

With A, right side facing and beginning with 1st marked st, PU and knit 1 st in corner st, then 45 more, for a total of 46 sts along length of rectangle. PU and knit 18 sts along width of rectangle, continue in this manner around—128 sts.

Work 10 rnds St st.

With B, work dec rnd as for bottom every 8th rnd, 4x. Work dec rnd every 6th rnd until 8 sts remain between corner sts along width of handbag (one time). Knit all other rounds.

K12, BO center 12 sts, k10, sl 2 sts tog as if to knit, k1, p2sso. K6, sl 2 sts tog as if to knit, k1, p2sso, k10. At this point, turn the piece and knit back and forth, instead of in the round. Keeping continuity of patt (in this case, stockinette stitch, so knit on RS, purl on WS) on these 28 sts, BO 6 sts each side 1x, BO 4 sts each side 1x, place 8 sts on hold for handles.

Join yarn and BO center 12 sts, k10, sl 2 sts tog as if to knit, k1, p2sso. K6, sl 2 sts tog as if to knit, k1, p2sso, k10. Keeping continuity of patt on these 28 sts, BO 6 sts each side 1x, BO 4 sts each side 1x. Keep rem 8 sts on needle for handles (do not cut yarn).

HANDLE

After binding off last 4 sts above, k3 more onto right needle and place on hold. Switch to DP needles and work 12 rows of 3 st I-cord, dec 1 st on 1st row. Place sts on hold.

Tip: See page 19 for a refresher on how to make I-cord.

Tip: Make a hand-written chart of which rows you will need to do decreases and the corresponding number of total stitches you should have in that row. Use your row counter to keep track of where you are in the pattern. Cross off each decrease row as you complete it. Always make decreases on odd-numbered rows.

Decrease rows are circled:

1, 2, 3, 4, 5, 6, 7, 8, ⑨, 10, 11, 12, 13, 14, 15, 16, ⑰, 18, 19, 20, 21, 22, 23, 24, ㉕, 26, 27, 28, 29, 30, 31, 32, ㉝, 34, 35, 36, 37, 38, ㊴, 40, 41, 42, 43, 44, ㊺, 46, 47, 48, 49, 50

Join yarn and work 12 rows of 3 st I-cord on rem 4 sts, dec 1 st on 1st row. Weave ends of I-cord together to form beginning of chain. Work alternating A and B 3 st I-cord for 22 rows forming a chain as you work by joining the ends of the I-cord together with the tapestry needle until 7 chains have been completed. With B, work beg of handle on 2nd side as 1st side.

Tip: See the Project in Progress on page 75 for further instructions on how to create the handle.

FINISHING

Edging
With B, work 1 rnd sc around opening of bag keeping crochet hook to inside of bag when approaching I-cord handles. Be sure to work 2 single chains in the space of I-cord handles.

Tip: See the Project in Progress on page 75 for further instructions on working the edging.

Flowers
With double pointed needles, work the following 3 st I-cord for flowers, stems and leaves.

Leave 8" tail of yarn at each end for attaching to the purse.

Stems: With C, work 2, 30-row, work 2, 24-row, work 2, 20-row.

Leaves: With C, work 12, 16-row.

Flowers: With each of D, E and F, work 2, 96-row.

Attach stems: Thread yarn at end of I-cord through tapestry needle. Place 30-row I-cord at center of purse attaching in 4 places. Place 24-row I-cord to the left of center stem attaching in 4 places. Place 20-row I-cord to the right of center stem attaching in 4 places.

Attach leaves: Fold 16-row I-cord in half, attach to stem, and 1 time at end of leaf.

Attach flowers: Weave flower petals on a tapestry needle. Draw tight and form a flower around the stem. Attach in several places to purse. Sew buttons at center.

Tip: See the Project in Progress on page 71 for further instructions on creating the flowers.

FELTING
Place handbag in a laundry bag or pillow protector. Wash in regular cycle with detergent in hot water, checking at regular intervals. If bag has not completely felted, reset wash cycle and continue agitation. Remove before spin cycle. Shape and stand to dry. Cut a piece of plastic the size of bottom rectangle, and place in bottom of bag for stability.

Tip: Consult *Basic Knitting* (Stackpole Books, 2004) for a full explanation of the felting process.

Knitting the Mitred Rectangle Bottom

A mitre (also spelled miter) is a term taken from carpentry. It's a joint that forms a corner, usually with both sides beveled at a 45-degree angle to form a 90-degree corner.

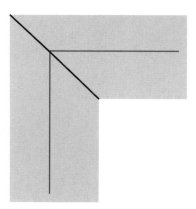

In knitting, mitred corners are used to create squares, rectangles, and other geometric shapes without adding bulky seams. When felted, as in this project, the mitred rectangle provides the additional strength and thickness needed to create the purse bottom.

Mitred corners are achieved through decreasing at the same point in each round of knitting. In this project, the decreases are worked until the stitches on the short sides of the rectangle are completely used up, then the stitches left from the long sides of the rectangle are joined together by binding off. The rectangle is knit in the round.

1. Cast on 128 stitches on a circular needle. Mark the 1st, 20th, 65th, and 84th stitches. The first blue marked stitch signifies the beginning of the round.

Tip: Marking individual stitches is different than placing a marker (pm) between stitches. When marking individual stitches, you will need to use a split marker or a brass pin that you can attach to the actual loop of the stitch. It is also helpful to use a different colored marker to signify the first stitch of the round.

2. Holding the needles with the first cast-on stitch in your left hand and the last cast-on stitch in your right hand, join the round by slipping the last cast-on from right needle to left needle.

5. Knit to within 1 stitch of the next marked corner.

3. Slip the stitch you just passed from the right needle along with the next stitch (the marked by stitch) together as if to knit.

6. Slip the stitch before the marked stitch and the marked stitch as if to knit, then knit the next stitch and then pass those 2 slipped stitches over the knit stitch.

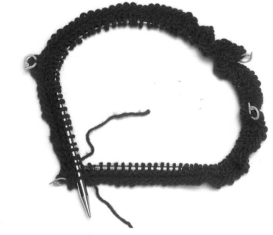

4. Knit the next stitch, and then pass those 2 slipped stitches over the knit stitch.

7. Continue Step 4 on the remaining corner stitches until you reach the first marked stitch. This completes Round 1.

8. Knit 1, then purl to the next marked stitch. Continue on the remaining corner stitches until you reach the stitch before the first marked stitch. This completes Round 2.

The stitches divided with 28 on each needle

9. Repeat these two rounds (Steps 3–7) until the mitred corners meet.

Note: When you start Round 1 again, you will slip the stitch before the marked stitch and the marked stitch to begin the round.

11. With right sides facing, bind off 28 stitches using the three-needle bind off (see page 17 for a refresher on this technique).

10. Complete this round, then knit 1 more stitch so the stitches can be divided evenly. Place the first 28 stitches on a spare needle.

The finished mitred rectangle

Embellishments

The I-cord embellishments are added to the purse prior to the felting process. You can refer to the illustration below to help guide you as you attach them to the fabric.

1. Using a tapestry needle, thread the end of the needle through the tail of one of the 30-row stems and position it at the center of the purse.

3. Running the threaded needle up through the center of the I-cord, further tack down the I-cord with 3 more evenly spaced stitches—2 in the middle and one at the top of the stem.

2. Tack the I-cord down by securing it with a stitch at the base of the stem.

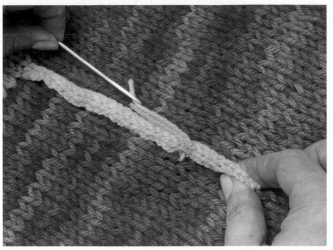

4. When you are finished tacking the stem down, run both yarn ends down through the middle of the I-cord and trim.

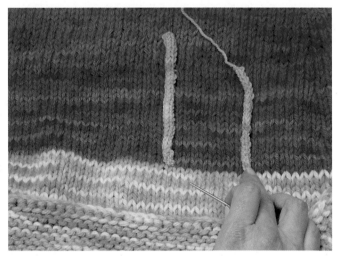

5. Repeat with the 20-row stem, placing it to the right of the middle stem.

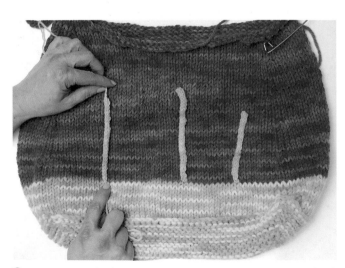

6. Repeat with the 24-row stem, placing it to the left of the middle stem.

7. Fold one of the 16-row leaves in half and position it at the base of the stem.

8. With one end of the I-cord, secure it at the base of the stem.

9. Run the threaded needle through the middle of the I-cord toward the tip of the leaf.

10. Tack down the tip of the leaf with another stitch.

11. Run the threaded needle back down to the base of the leaf and tack down.

12. Secure the two loose ends of yarn on the I-cord by tying them in a knot at the base of the leaf. Thread both ends through the needle, run through the middle of the I-cord to the tip of the leaf and trim (see Step 4).

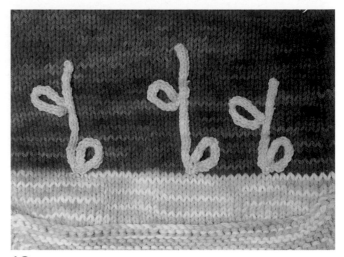

13. Repeat with five other leaves.

14. Weave the tapestry needle through one of the 96-row flowers.

15. Shape the piece of I-cord into flower petals as shown in the illustration. No need to be exact; use your own creativity to make a flower you like.

17. With the same thread, sew a button at the center of the flower.

16. Attach the flower to the top of one of the stems. Start by connecting the last and first petals, then make a stitch at the base of each petal in between.

The finished secured flower

18. Tie the ends of the yarn in a knot at the back of the flower, run through to the end of the flower and trim.

19. Repeat for the other two flowers.

20. Repeat Steps 1–19 on the back side of the purse, varying the color arrangement as desired.

Creating the Handle and Working the Edging
The chain-link handle is made of I-cord.

1. After you have bound off the last 4 stitches in the purse, knit 3 more stitches onto the right needle, giving you 4 stitches on the needle. Place these stitches on hold.

2. Transfer the remaining 4 stitches to a double pointed needle.

Beaver Meadows Felted Purse

3. Work 12 rows of 3-stitch I-cord, decreasing 1 stitch on the first row. Leave the stitches on the needle.

4. Transfer the 4 stitches on hold to a double pointed needle and join another ball of yarn (B).

5. Repeat Step 3 to create a second 12-row piece of I-cord to match the first.

6. When finished with the second piece of I-cord, graft the two pieces together using Kitchener stitch (see page 20).

7. With A, work a 22-row, 3-stitch I-cord. When finished, thread the piece through the loop created in Steps 1–6.

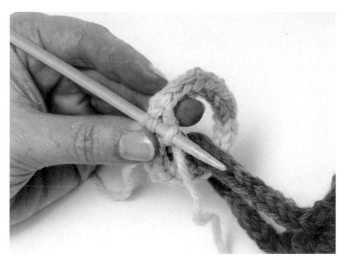

8. You will graft the live stitches to the bound-off stitches: Place the bound-off stitches above the live stitches on the DP needle.

9. Cut the tail of the live stitches, leaving an 8-inch tail to thread through a tapestry needle.

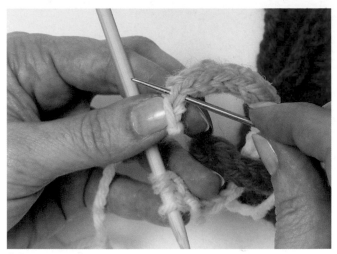

10. Insert the tapestry needle up through the first stitch on the bound-off edge and pull the yarn through.

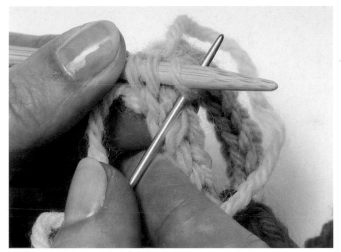

11. Insert the tapestry needle into the first live stitch on the needle as if to knit.

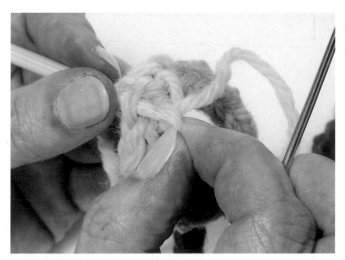

12. Drop the stitch off the needle.

13. Insert the tapestry needle into the next live stitch on the needle as if to purl. Leave the stitch on the needle.

14. Repeat Steps 10–13 until all the stitches are grafted together.

15. Weave the ends through the I-cord and trim.

16. Repeat Steps 7–15, alternating Colors A and B to add a total of 7 links to the chain (not including the anchor link).

17. Repeat Steps 1–6 to create the second anchor link and place the last chain link through the open end.

18. Graft the live stitches together using Kitchener stitch as in Step 6.

The finished chain handle

With B, work 1 rnd single chain around opening of bag keeping crochet hook to inside of bag when approaching I-cord handles. Be sure to work 2 single chains in the space of I-cord handles.

19. Join a ball of B. Insert the crochet hook into the stitch just to the left of the anchor loop of the handle.

20. Work a round of single chain around the opening of the bag.

21. As you reach the anchor loop of the handle, move the crochet hook to the inside of the bag.

The finished single chain stitches on the inside of the anchor loop of the handle

22. Continue the single chain around the other side of the bag and inside the other anchor loop to complete the round.

The finished single chain edging

7

Big Rock Socks

Gauge: 26 sts and 36 rows to 4"
in St st on US 3 needle
(or size to obtain gauge)

Materials:

DK weight Wool/Nylon
Blend (3) (200 yds/
skein), 1 skein Color A,
1 skein Color B

US 3 Double Pointed
Needles (set of 4)

US 5 Needle (any type)

Tapestry Needle

Sample knit in Twin Twist
(92% Wool, 8% Nylon),
Color A, Pacific; Color B,
Parrot

Sometimes mistakenly referred to as "Fair Isle knitting," (see sidebar on page 84) the technique used in these colorful socks is more accurately known as stranded color knitting, because the strand of second color is carried along the back of the garment. Don't be intimidated by the thought of knitting with two colors at the same time; after a few rows of practicing the technique you will find that your dexterity increases rapidly. The Skill Workshop will guide you through learning to knit with yarn in both hands—the most efficient way to achieve stranded color knitting.

LEG

With A and larger needle, CO 56 sts. Divide sts onto 3 smaller double pointed needles with 18, 20, 18 sts on each needle respectively. Join and purl 1 row.

Set up bi-color rib: [k2A, k2B] around.

Tip: When adding the second color, simply loop the end of the second skein over the needle and pull through on the first stitch; there is no need to knot or otherwise secure. Make sure to leave a long enough tail that you can securely weave in when finished. See the Skill Workshop on page 84 for more tips on stranded color knitting technique.

Bi-color rib: [p2B, k2A] around. Work 7 more rnds (for a total of 8 rnds).

With A, k4 rnds.

Tip: When knitting multiple (fewer than 8) rows of a single color, do not cut the unused color. Carry it along the side, securing it on every other row on the beginning stitch of the round by working a carry. See the Skill Workshop on page 84 for details on how to do this.

With B, k1 rnd, p1 rnd.

In addition to the written patterns on page 82, here is a chart of the three patterns used in the Big Rock Socks. See the Skill Workshop on page 63 for guidance on how to read a graph.

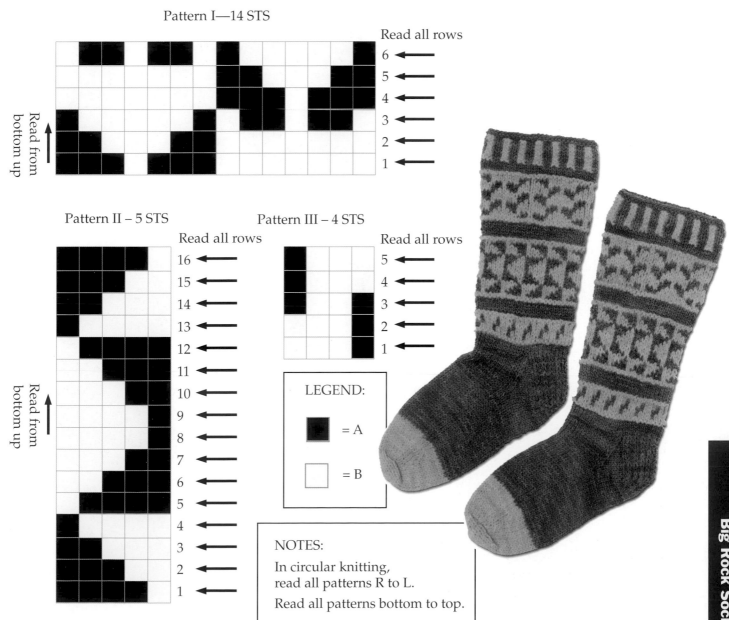

Pattern I—14 STS

Read all rows

Read from bottom up

Pattern II – 5 STS

Read all rows

Read from bottom up

Pattern III – 4 STS

Read all rows

LEGEND:

■ = A

☐ = B

NOTES:

In circular knitting, read all patterns R to L.

Read all patterns bottom to top.

PATTERN I

Rnd 1: * k7B, k3A, k1B, k3A; rep from * around.

Rnd 2: * k7B, k2A, k3B, k2A; rep from * around.

Rnd 3: * k1B, k2A, k1B, k2A, k1B, k1A, k5B, k1A; rep from * around.

Rnd 4: * k3A, k1B, k3A, k7B; rep from * around.

Rnd 5: * k2A, k3B, k2A, k7B; rep from * around.

Rnd 6: * k1A, k5B, k1A, k1B, k2A, k1B, k2A, k1B; rep from * around.

Work patt 1 2x. Work Rnd 1 of patt 1.

Tip: To help remember which color is "A" and which is "B," write down on a slip of paper: "A = purple" and "B = orange."

Tip: Each round has a total of 14 sts between the asterisks. This may help when starting out each round on Needles 1 and 3 (you should have 4 stitches left on Needle 1 when you finish the first repeat and 14 stitches left on Needle 3 when you start the last one).

With B, k1 rnd, p1 rnd.
With A, k6 rnds dec 6 sts on 1st rnd—50 sts.
With B, k1 rnd, p1 rnd.

PATTERN II

Rnd 1: * k1B, k4A; rep from * around.
Rnd 2: * k2B, k3A; rep from * around.
Rnd 3: * k3B, k2A; rep from * around.
Rnd 4: * k4B, k1A; rep from * around.
Rnd 5: * k4A, k1B; rep from * around.
Rnd 6: * k3A, k2B; rep from * around.
Rnd 7: * k2A, k3B; rep from * around.
Rnd 8: * k1A, k4B; rep from * around.
Rnd 9: * k1A, k4B; rep from * around.
Rnd 10: * k2A, k3B; rep from * around.
Rnd 11: * k3A, k2B; rep from * around.
Rnd 12: * k4A, k1B; rep from * around.
Rnd 13: * k4B, k1A; rep from * around.
Rnd 14: * k3B, k2A; rep from * around.
Rnd 15: * k2B, k3A; rep from * around.
Rnd 16: * k1B, k4A; rep from * around.
Work patt 2 1x.
With B, k1 rnd, p1 rnd.
With A, k6 rnds dec 2 sts on 1st rnd—48 sts, 16 sts on each needle.
With B, k1 rnd, p1 rnd.

PATTERN III

Rnd 1: * k1A, k3B; rep from * around.
Rnd 2: * k1A, k3B; rep from * around.
Rnd 3: * k1A, k2B, k1A; rep from * around.
Rnd 4: * k3B, k1A; rep from * around.
Rnd 5: * k3B, k1A; rep from * around.
Work patt 3 1x.
With B, k1 rnd, p1 rnd.
With A, k4 rnds.

HEEL

K12 (heel). Place next 24 sts on one needle. Place remaining 12 sts with 1st 12 heel sts.

Row 1: (WS) sl1, purl to end of row. Row 2: [sl1, k1] to end of row. Repeat the last two rows until 22 total rows have been completed.

Note: Row 2 creates a reinforced heel.

TO TURN HEEL
(continue heel reinforcement on right side rows)

Row 1: (WS) p14, p2tog, p1, turn.
Row 2: sl1, k5, k2togtbl, k1, turn.
Row 3: sl1, p6, p2tog, p1, turn.
Row 4: sl1, k7, k2togtbl, k1, turn.
Row 5: sl1, p8, p2tog, p1, turn.
Row 6: sl1, k9, k2togtbl, k1, turn.
Row 7: sl1, p10, p2tog, turn.
Row 8: sl1, k11, k2togtbl, k1, turn.
Row 9: sl1, p12, p2tog.
Row 10: sl1, k12, k2togtbl.

GUSSET

(Discontinue heel reinforcement): (RS) Pick up and k12 sts along right side of heel with extra needle. With another needle, k24 instep sts. With another needle, pick up and k12 sts up other side of heel. Continue to knit 7 sts from heel sts. Place remaining 7 sts on the 1st needle. Needles should contain 19, 24, 19 sts. Knit 1 rnd. Decrease next rnd as follows: k to last 3 sts on 1st needle, k2tog, k1; k24 sts on 2nd needle; k1, k2togtbl, k to end of rnd on 3rd needle. Continue last row until 12 sts remain on 1st and 3rd needles.

FOOT

Work rnds in St st until sock measures 3" from finished length.

TOE

Next (dec) rnd: With B, k to last 3 sts on 1st needle, k2tog, k1; k1, k2togtbl, k to last 3 sts, k2tog, k1 on 2nd needle; k1, k2togtbl, k to end of rnd on 3rd needle. K3 rnds. Work dec rnd. K3 rnds. Work dec rnd. K2 rnds. Work dec rnd. K2 rnds. Work dec rnd. K1 rnd. Work dec rnd. K1 rnd. Work dec rnd, 2x. K4 sts from 1st to 3rd needle. Weave 8 sts on one needle with 8 sts from the other needle.

Tip: See page 20 for a refresher on how to weave stitches together using Kitchener stitch.

Big Rock Socks

Stranded color knitting, often mistakenly referred to as Fair Isle knitting, involves knitting with two colors of yarn at once, carrying the unused color across the back of the work until you need it again. To avoid long strands of yarn across the back of the garment, the yarn is usually carried, or wrapped, by securing it with the yarn currently being worked. This also prevents the second color from showing through the front of the piece and prevents the finished piece from puckering.

This Skill Workshop will teach you the basic technique of stranded color knitting. Since the swatch is knit in the flat, you will learn how to both knit and purl in this fashion, wrapping the carries as you go. Since the Big Rock Socks are knit in the round, you will only need to do stranded color knitting on the knit stitches.

What Is Fair Isle Knitting?

Fair Isle knitting is a specific type of stranded color knitting that originated on (you guessed it) Fair Isle, off the coast of Scotland. True Fair Isle knitting uses only Shetland wool and typically is characterized by color changes in both the foreground and background colors. "X" and "O" motifs are common. Stranded color knitting uses the same two-handed technique but encompasses patterns of all kinds.

For this swatch, you will practice by knitting Pattern I from the Big Rock Socks. Note, however, that since it will be knit in the flat rather than in the round, you will need to work the even rows in purl stitch in the reverse order:

Rnd 1: k7B, k3A, k1B, k3A
Rnd 2: p2A, p3B, p2A, p7B
Rnd 3: k1B, k2A, k1B, k2A, k1B, k1A, k5B, k1A
Rnd 4: p7B, p3A, p1B, p3A
Rnd 5: k2A, k3B, k2A, k7B
Rnd 6: p1B, p2A, p1B, p2A, p1B, p1A, p5B, p1A

English vs. Continental Knitting Methods

Although the majority of knitters in North America and Great Britain knit by holding the working yarn in their right hands (known as the English method), in Germany, France, and most other European countries, knitters hold the working yarn in their left hand (know as the Continental method). English-style knitters "throw" the yarn over the needle, while Continental-style knitters "pick" the yarn through the loop. Both methods produce the same basic end product, so the choice of method is a personal one that depends mainly on how you were first taught to knit. Some knitters prefer the Continental style, as it is faster and more efficient than the English style. In stranded color knitting, you will gradually become proficient in both styles, although your non-dominant style will feel awkward and uncoordinated at first.

English-style knitting

Continental-style knitting

ROUND 1: KNIT SIDE

1. Cast on 18 stitches. Work 2 garter stitch edge stitches on either side of the swatch (all edge stitches should be knit in B). Knit 4 rows of stockinette stitch.

2. As you begin Round 1, hold Color A (blue) in your left hand and Color B (gold) in your right hand.

3. With B tacked down on the right needle with your right thumb, knit the 2 garter stitch edge stitches with A.

4. Insert the right needle into the next stitch and prepare to introduce B by tacking it down between your left thumb on the front of the swatch and your left middle finger on the back of the swatch. Wrap the working end around your right index finger to establish tension.

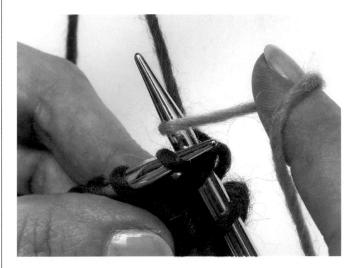

5. Wrap B around the left needle as to knit (English style) and knit the stitch.

6. Knit the next stitch the same way.

7. On the third stitch, you will work a carry. Insert the needle into the stitch as to prepare to knit, then pull A over the top of the right needle, keeping the tension nice and tight with your left index finger.

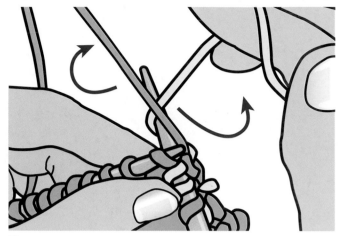

8. Now, wrap B around the right needle as if to knit, keeping A overtop of the right needle.

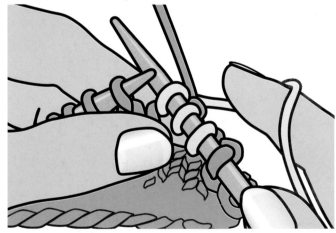

9. Back out A, pulling through only B, leaving A at the back, anchored to the stitch.

10. Knit the fourth stitch with B.

The completed carry on the sixth stitch

The carry worked on the third stitch from the back of the swatch

12. Work the seventh stitch with B.

11. Knit the fifth stitch, and then on the sixth stitch, work another carry.

13. To work the eighth stitch with A, insert the needle into the next stitch as if to knit and then wrap the yarn with the left hand as to knit Continental style.

As you prepare to knit the eighth stitch with A, it is important to maintain tension with B.

14. Knit the stitch Continental style.

Tip: When working with the yarn in your left hand, you should be "picking" the yarn through the stitch (Continental style); when holding the yarn in your right hand, you should be "throwing" it around the needle, then pulling through (English style).

15. Knit the ninth stitch with A.

16. Work a carry on the tenth stitch, but this time carrying B by backing out A, pulling through only B.

Note: You need to work a carry after knitting 3 stitches in a new color, so since you switched from B to A on stitch 7, you will work the carry on stitch 10.

17. Knit stitch 11 with B, remembering to maintain proper tension on A with your left hand.

18. Switch back to A and knit stitches 12, 13, and 14, working a carry on stitch 14.

19. Knit the 2 edge stitches in B.

The right side of finished Round 1

The wrong side of finished Round 1, showing the carries

1. Knit the 2 edge stitches in A, then purl stitches 1 and 2 of the pattern. Remember, since you are holding A in your left hand, you will need to purl Continental style.

2. On stitch 3, switch to B and purl the next stitch English style.

3. Purl stitch 4.

Big Rock Socks

4. On stitch 5, you will work the carry. First, insert the right needle into the next stitch as if to purl.

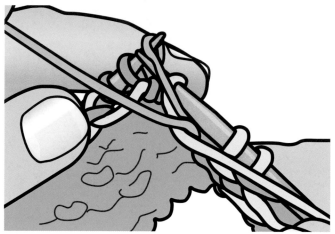

6. Now back A out and pull through only B.

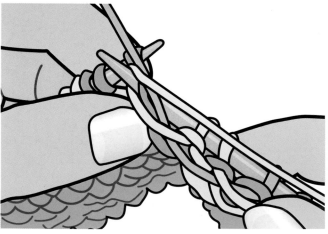

The completed carry on stitch 5

5. Next, keeping A overtop, wrap B underneath as if to purl (English style).

7. Switch to A and purl stitches 6 and 7.

8. Switch to B and purl stitches 8 and 9, then work a carry on stitch 10.

The completed carry on stitch 10

9. Purl stitches 11 and 12 with B and then work another carry on stitch 13.

10. Purl stitch 14 of the pattern.

11. Knit the two edge stitches in B.

The wrong side of completed Round 2, showing the carries

The right side of completed Round 2

The wrong side of completed Round 6, showing the carries

The right side of completed Round 6

8

Tionesta Lake Throw

Gauge: 20 sts and 28 rows to 7" in patt and color sequence on US 13 (or size to obtain gauge)

Measurements: 60" x 58"

Materials:

Medium weight Cotton/Rayon Blend, 200 yds/skein (4), 5 skeins

Lightweight Rayon, 200 yds/skein (3), 5 skeins

Medium weight Cotton Blend, 200 yds/skein (4), 5 skeins

Bulky weight Mohair Blend, 200 yds/skein (5), 2 skeins—1 each of 2 different colors

US 13 32" Circular Needle (or size to obtain gauge)

Sample knit in

A: Pop (Cellulose Blend)

B: Cameo (100% Rayon) and Helix (97% Cotton, 3% Nylon) held together

C: Miss Mohair (78% Mohair, 13% Wool, 9% Nylon)

D: Miss Mohair (78% Mohair, 13% Wool, 9% Nylon)

The selection of colors and textures of yarn is one of the most creative aspects of knitting. Yarns come in just about every color of the spectrum and range in texture from the most delicate mohairs to the chunkiest wools. A knitter can create true artistry by selectively combining colors and textures to the greatest effect. Designed with the simplest of patterns, this throw is the perfect introduction to creating artistry with yarn. But mastering the skill is subjective: no one choice of colors or textural patterns is more correct than another. Only with practice will you learn which choices produce the finished results that are most pleasing to you.

PATTERN

Row 1: [k5, p5] to last 5 sts, k5.
This row worked RS and WS.

COLOR SEQUENCE

Row 1 and 2: A
Row 3 and 4: B
Row 5 and 6: A
Row 7 and 8: B
Row 9 and 10: C
Row 11 and 12: A
Row 13 and 14: B
Row 15 and 16: A
Row 17 and 18: B
Row 19 and 20: D
Row 21 and 22: A
Row 23 and 24: B
These 24 rows form color sequence.

THROW

CO 175 sts. Work patt in color sequence until piece measures 58" slightly stretched. To create fringe, cut yarn at the end of each row, leaving a 6- to 8-inch tail and securing it to the previous row's tail with an overhand knot (see page 96). BO loosely.

Tip: The throw will appear symmetrical if knitter ends with Row 8 of color sequence.

SKILL WORKSHOP: SWATCHING FOR TEXTURE AND COLOR

The secret to this project's beauty is not in the pattern, which is a simple broken rib repeated throughout the throw, but in the choice of colors and textures of the yarn in which it is knitted. In this project, there are four different types of yarn chosen: a cellulose blend, two colors of mohair, and a rayon yarn held together with a cotton/nylon blend. The rayon and cotton/nylon blend are held together so that their combined weight will match that of the other yarns in the project.

This Skill Workshop will show, briefly, how these yarns combine following the pattern above. You can create similar swatches when working on your own projects to experiment with combining different colors and textures of yarn.

1. Cast on 15 stitches with A. Knit Rows 1 and 2 of the pattern. Cut the yarn at the end of each row, leaving a 6- to 8-inch tail. As you join yarn at the beginning of each row, do not secure it with a knot; simply pin down the loose yarn with your finger and knit the first few stitches carefully. (This will also give you more flexibility to adjust the length of the tail to match the previous ones.) You will be knotting the tails of the yarns below to secure the fringe (see Step 5).

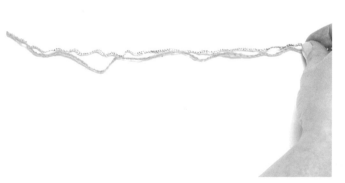

2. Prepare B by holding the rayon yarn and cotton blend together.

3. Knit Rows 3 and 4 with B, holding the two yarns together. Don't forget to cut the yarn at the end of each row for the fringe.

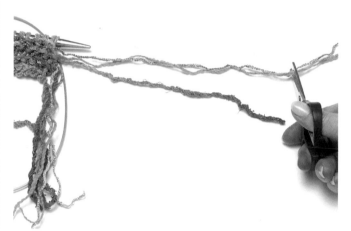

4. Knit Rows 5 and 6 with A, then 7 and 8 with B, cutting the yarn at the end of each row for the fringe.

5. At the end of Row 8, tie the tail of this row together with the tail from Row 6 (A) with a loose overhand knot. Go back and secure previous rows' tails in the same fashion and continue to do so moving forward.

6. Following the pattern, knit Rows 9 and 10 with C, the blue mohair blend, followed by Rows 11 and 12 with A.

The swatch at the end of Row 8, with A and B. Notice how the size of the ball of A is roughly equal to the size of the two balls that make up B.

The swatch at the end of Row 12, with combined yarns so far

7. Knit Rows 13–18 with B, A, and B as written, then introduce D, the multicolor mohair blend, in Rows 19 and 20.

The swatch with all 5 yarns introduced

8. Complete the swatch with Rows 21–24, using A and B. Bind off loosely.

The finished swatch

9

Watson Crossing Sweater

Gauge: 9.5 sts and 12 rows to 4" in St st on US 15 or size to obtain gauge

Measurements:

Finished Bust: 38.75 (40, 42)"

Finished Length: 20 (21, 21.5)"

Materials:

Bulky weight Mohair Blend, 200 yards **[5]** 2 (3, 3) skeins

Lightweight Rayon Blend, 200 yards **[3]** 2 (3, 3) skeins

Lightweight Wool Blend, 200 yards **[3]** 3 (3, 3) skeins

US 15 Circular Needle (or size to obtain gauge)

US 15 Double Pointed Needles (for I-Cord)

Sample knit in

A: Miss Mohair (78% Mohair, 13% Wool, 9% Nylon), Storm's End

B: Shaggy (75% Rayon, 25% Polyester), Lottery

C: Tilly (92% Wool, 8% Nylon), Lottery

One of the most critical aspects of a knitted garment is the neckline. The best-knit backs, fronts, and sleeves can be compromised if the shape of the neck doesn't look just right. Don't let this tragedy befall your first complex knitted garment. The Skill Workshop in this project provides tips and advice on how to knit a flawless neckline. The sweater is knit with three strands held together, which not only produces a rich, thick texture, but also helps to make the project go much more quickly. So if you're ready to take on a multi-piece garment and want to do it right, this project is for you!

BODY

Using long-tail CO, loosely CO 150 (155, 160) sts. Work edging until 1 st remains on needle.

EDGING

Row 1 (WS): BO 2 sts * replace st to left-hand needle, [CO 2 sts, BO 2 sts, replace st to left-hand needle] 3x, CO 2 sts, BO 6 sts; rep from * to end.

Tip: Practice the edging technique on scrap yarn before attempting it with the project yarn. It's simple once you get the hang of it, but ripping out cast-off stitches with mohair yarn is something you want to avoid.

Leave the st on the needle and continue by picking up 149 (154, 159) more sts along original cast on edge. Purl 1 row slipping 1st st and keeping 5 edge sts in gar st at each end.

Decrease Row: sl 1st st and dec 10 sts evenly between 5 gar st edge sts—140 (145, 150) sts.

Tip: You can figure out how to evenly distribute the decrease stitches by dividing the finished number of stitches by the number you want to decrease and then splitting that number subtracting 2 to see how many stitches you need to knit before decreasing. For example, for the first decrease row above:

140 divided by 10 = 14.

14 minus 2 = 12.

So, knit 12, then knit 2 together.

Work 3 rows St st keeping the 5 edge sts in gar st and continuing to slip the 1st st in each row.

Decrease Row: As est, dec 10 sts evenly—130 (135, 140) sts.

As est, work 3 rows St st.

Decrease Row: As est, dec 10 sts evenly—120 (125, 130) sts.

As est, work 3 rows St st.

Decrease Row: As est, dec 10 sts evenly—110 (115, 120) sts.

As est, work 3 rows st st.

Decrease Row: As est, dec 10 sts evenly—100 (105, 110) sts.

As est, work 3 rows St st.

Decrease Row: As est, dec 8 (9, 10) sts evenly—92 (96, 100) sts.

As est, work 3 rows St st.

Work even until piece measures 10.5 (11, 11.5)". Cut yarn.

Divide sts for fronts and back: Place the first 23 (24, 25) sts on a holder (right front). Keep the next 46 (48, 50) sts on the needle (back). Place the last 23 (24, 25) sts on another holder (left front).

BACK

Join new yarn for a right side row and continue in St st. Work armhole decreases as follows: Dec 1 st each side every other row 15x—16 (18, 20) sts.

Tip: Work the decreases like this: k1, ssk to the last 3 sts, k2tog, k1. Purl even rows.

When piece measures 20 (21, 22.5)", BO.

FRONTS

Place both fronts on the needle and work together. Join the previous ball of yarn to work the right front; join a second ball to work the left front. Continue in St st. Work armhole shaping as for back, AT THE SAME TIME, dec 1 st each neck edge every other row, 2 (3, 4)x—19 (18, 17) sts.

Note: Stop slipping the 1st st at neck edge at this point.

Tip: The above corresponds to Rows 1–4 of the ANNA chart in the Skill Workshop on page 101. See the Skill Workshop for further illustration of how to work both fronts on the needle together.

Dec 1 st each neck edge every 4th row 5x. Continue armhole dec until 1 st remains. Fasten off.

TIPS

- It's easy to get confused about whether you are working the armhole or the neck edge. Pick up the garment and look at it to help figure it out.
- As you get closer to finishing each front (beyond Row 21 of the ANNA chart on page 101), it may be easier to knit one side at a time to completion rather than jumping back and forth between the left and right fronts.

SLEEVES

Using long-tail CO, CO 26 (30, 34) sts. Knit 1 row. Work 2 rows St st. Continue in St st inc 1 st each side every 4th row 3x—32 (36, 40) sts. Work until piece measures 6 (7, 8)". Work armhole dec as for back until 4 (6, 10) sts remain.

Small Size Only:

Next row: ssk, k2tog.

Next row: Purl.

Next row: k2tog. Fasten off.

Medium and Large Size Only:

BO.

FINISHING

Sew sleeve seams. Sew in sleeves.

COLLAR

With RS facing and beginning at right v-neck, PU and knit 30 (36, 40) sts to back. PU and knit 16 (18, 20) sts across back. PU and knit 30 (36, 40) sts down left front. Purl 1 row. Purl 1 row inc 14 (10, 10) sts evenly. Purl 1 row. Work Row 2 of edging. Fasten off.

I-CORD EDGING

CO 2 sts. Work I-cord for desired length of button loop. With RS facing at right neck, begin working attached 2 st I-cord around to left front. K2tog. Fasten off.

Tip: See page 19 for a refresher on how to make I-cord.

Keeping track of armhole and neck decreases can be a logistical challenge. In this sweater, you need to work the armhole decreases as you did for the back at the same time you work a different schedule of decreases along the neckline of the garment.

To keep this straight, let ANNA help. ANNA stands for "armhole, neck, neck, armhole," and refers to the order in which the decreases are worked. An ANNA chart is a simple graphical representation of where the decreases should be placed. This Skill Workshop will introduce the ANNA chart on swatches that simulate the two fronts of the Watson Crossing sweater. It will also help to illustrate how to work both fronts of the sweater on the needle at the same time.

The chart you will follow is reproduced below:

	A	N	N	A
1 (RS)	#	#	#	#
3	#	#	#	#
5	#	#	#	#
7	#	-	-	#
9	#	#	#	#
11	#	-	-	#
13	#	#	#	#
15	#	-	-	#
17	#	#	#	#
19	#	-	-	#
21	#	#	#	#

A = armhole   N = neck   # = decrease   - = work even

All even rows are purled. This example is for the smallest size only.

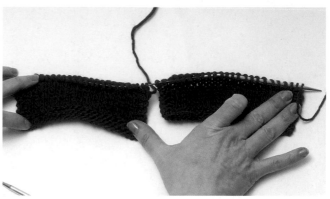

1. On a 32–36" circular needle, cast on two swatches with 24 stitches each, using a separate ball of yarn for the second swatch. Knit 4 rows of garter stitch border on each. Work 8 rows of stockinette stitch, working the first 2 and last 2 stitches of each swatch in garter stitch.

2. Starting with Row 1 of the ANNA chart, you will work a decrease at the right armhole edge. Although the chart does not specify, all right armhole decreases should be ssk.

3. When you reach the neck edge of the right swatch, work another decrease. All right neck decreases should be k2tog.

4. Pick up the second ball of yarn to start working the left swatch.

5. Still on Row 1 of the ANNA chart, work the neck decrease on the left swatch. All left neck decreases should be ssk.

6. When you reach the armhole edge of the left swatch, work another decrease. All left armhole decreases should be k2tog. This completes Row 1 of the ANNA chart.

7. Purl across the backs of both swatches to complete Row 2.

8. Work Row 3 of the chart, which is the same as Row 1, with decreases at both the armhole and neck edges.

9. Purl across the back sides of both swatches to complete Row 4, then work Row 5, another row with decreases at both armhole and neck edges. This row is the first of the five times of neck decreases worked every 4th row (Dec 1 st each neck edge every 4th row 5x).

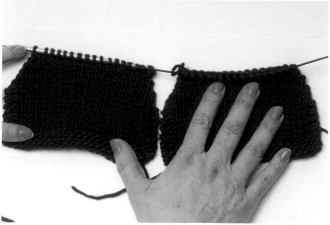

10. Purl across the back of both swatches to complete Row 6, then work Row 7, which calls for a decrease only at the armhole edges; work both neck edges even.

11. Purl across the back of both swatches to complete Row 8, then work Row 9, which again calls for decreases at both the armhole and neck edges. This row is the second of the five times of neck decreases worked every 4th row.

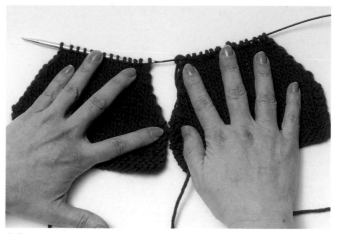

12. Purl across the back of both swatches to complete Row 10, then work Row 11, which calls for a decrease only at the armhole edges; work both neck edges even.

13. Continue in this fashion, working the decreases as indicated in the chart. Rows 13–21 of the chart complete the remainder of the neck decreases. After this point you will work the armhole decreases only until you have just one stitch remaining.

10

Saybrook Neck Warmer and Wrist Warmers

Gauge: 15 sts and 20 rows to 4" in st st on US 10 needles (or size to obtain gauge)

Measurements:

Neck Warmer:
23" around x 9½" length

Wrist Warmers:
8" around x 6½" length

Materials:

Bulky weight Cellulose Blend (5) 200 yds/skein, 1 skein

US 10 Circular Needle (or size to obtain gauge)

US 10 6" Double Pointed Needles (set of four)

Size B Crochet Hook

Cable Needle

48 beads with a 3 mm opening

Samples knit in Double Deal (65% Cotton, 35% Rayon) Colors: Naples (shown at left); Jackpot (page 105–106)

Abbreviations (specific to this pattern):

bead 1: Using a crochet hook, insert hook through bead, pull next stitch on left-hand needle through bead and return to LH needle, k1.

C3L: Place next stitch on cable needle and hold at front of work. Knit next 2 stitches. Knit stitch from cable needle.

C3R: Place next 2 stitches on cable needle and hold at back of work. Knit next stitch. Knit 2 stitches from cable needle.

Beads lend an extra element of creativity and visual interest to a knitted garment, enhancing the color and texture of the finished piece. Knitting with beads is a deceptively simple process; the end result can make even simple patterns look more challenging. This trendy neck warmer and matching wrist warmers provide an ideal introduction to knitting with beads. Heavier cellulose yarn and larger-gauge beads make it easy to focus on the technique. Have fun with your bead choice for the project; by selecting contrasting colors or interesting patterns, you can add a totally different look to the finished garment.

NECK WARMER

CO 117 sts. PM and join.

Rnd 1: * k2, sl1, k1, psso, sl2, k3tog, psso, k2tog, k2; rep from * around—63 sts.

Rnd 2: * k3, yo, bead 1, yo, k3; rep from * around—81 sts.

Rnd 3: * yo, k2, sl1, k1, psso, k1, k2tog, k2; rep from * around—72 sts.

Rnd 4: * bead 1, yo, k2, yo, k3, yo, k2, yo; rep from * around—108 sts.

Rnd 5: * k1, yo, k1, yo, sl1, k1, psso, k1, sl1, k2tog, psso, k1, k2tog, yo, k1, yo; rep from * around—108 sts.

Rnd 6: Knit.

Rnd 7: * k4, yo, sl2, k3tog, psso, yo, k3; rep from * around—90 sts.

Rnd 8: Knit.

Rnd 9: Purl.

Rnd 10: * k8, k2tog; rep from * around—81 sts.

Rnd 11: Purl.

Rnd 12: * p1, k6, p2; rep from * around.

Rnd 13: Same as Rnd 12.

Rnd 14: Same as Rnd 12.

Rnd 15: Same as Rnd 12.

Rnd 16: * p1, C3L, C3R, p2; rep from * around.

Rnd 17: Same as Rnd 12.

Rnd 18: Same as Rnd 16.

Rnd 19: Same as Rnd 12.

Rnd 20: Same as Rnd 16.

Rnd 21: Same as Rnd 12.

Rnd 22–31: Same as Rnds 12—21.

Rnd 32–35: Same as Rnd 12.

Rnd 36: Purl.

Place sts on hold.

CO 117 sts. PM and join.

Work Rnds 1–8.

Rnd 9: * p8, p2tog; rep from * around—81 sts.

Weave 81 sts to 81 sts on hold using Kitchener stitch (see page 20).

Tip: For Row 2: Be sure not to let the yo slip off your right needle as you do the bead 1. Also, don't forget the yo that follows the bead 1. Make sure to count your stitches at the end of each round to make sure you haven't missed any before moving on to the next row.

WRIST WARMERS

CO 39 sts. PM and join.

Rnd 1: * k2, sl1, k1, psso, sl2, k3tog, psso, k2tog, k2; rep from * around—21 sts

Rnd 2: * k3, yo, bead 1, yo, k3; rep from * around—27 sts.

Rnd 3: * yo, k2, sl1, k1, psso, k1, k2tog, k2; rep from * around—24 sts.

Rnd 4: * bead 1, yo, k2, yo, k3, yo, k2, yo; rep from * around—36 sts.

Rnd 5: * k1, yo, k1, yo, sl1, k1, psso, k1, sl1, k2tog, psso, k1, k2tog, yo, k1, yo; rep from * around—36 sts.

Rnd 6: Knit.

Rnd 7: * k4, yo, sl2, k3tog, psso, yo, k3; rep from * around—30 sts.

Rnd 8: Knit.

Rnd 9: Purl.

Rnd 10: * k8, k2tog; rep from * around—27 sts.

Rnd 11: Purl.

Rnd 12: * p1, k6, p2; rep from * around.

Rnd 13: Same as Rnd 12.

Rnd 14: Same as Rnd 12.

Rnd 15: Same as Rnd 12.

Rnd 16: * p1, C3L, C3R, p2; rep from * around.

Rnd 17: Same as Rnd 12.

Rnd 18: Same as Rnd 16.

Rnd 19: Same as Rnd 12.

Rnd 20: Same as Rnd 16.

Rnd 21–26: Same as Rnd 12.

Rnd 27: k1, BO 6, knit to end.

Rnd 28: p1, turn, CO6, turn, P2, purl to end.

Rnd 29: Knit.

Rnd 30: Purl.

Rnd 31: Knit.

Rnd 32: Purl.

BO loosely in pattern.

Adding beads to a knitted garment requires a crochet hook that you will use to pull the yarn through the bead before knitting a stitch on top of it to secure it. You will need to make sure that the hook you choose is small enough to pass completely through the opening in the bead. You may want to take one of your beads along when you shop for your crochet hook (or your hook when you shop for beads) to ensure a proper fit.

3. Gently pull the loop through the bead. Pull tightly enough only to pass the loop completely through the bead.

1. Following the pattern, knit up to the point at which you want to add a bead. Gently put down your knitting and pick up the crochet hook. Pass the hook through the opening in the bead.

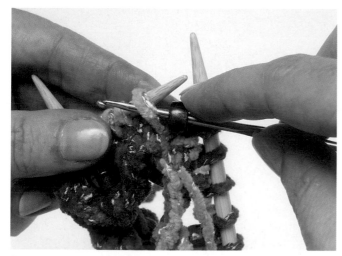

2. Pick your knitting back up, holding the crochet hook in your right hand and supporting the knitting in your left, pass the hook under the top of the next loop on your left needle.

4. Transfer the loop with the bead from the crochet hook back onto the left needle.

The finished beaded stitch

5. Knit this stitch (on top of the bead) to secure it and pass it off the left needle as usual.

Appendices

Knitting Abbreviations Master List

Following is a list of knitting abbreviations used by yarn industry designers and publishers. The most commonly used abbreviations are highlighted. In addition, designers and publishers may use special abbreviations in a pattern, which you might not find on this list. Generally, a definition of special abbreviations is given at the beginning of a book or pattern.

Abbreviation	Description
[ ]	work instructions within brackets as many times as directed
( )	work instructions within parentheses in the place directed
* *	repeat instructions following the asterisks as directed
*	repeat instructions following the single asterisk as directed
"	inch(es)
alt	alternate
approx	approximately
beg	begin/beginning
bet	between
BO	bind off
CA	color A
CB	color B
CC	contrasting color
cm	centimeter(s)
cn	cable needle
CO	cast on
cont	continue
dec	decrease/decreases/decreasing
dpn	double pointed needle(s)
fl	front loop(s)
foll	follow/follows/following
g	gram
inc	increase/increases/increasing
k or **K**	knit
k2tog	knit 2 stitches together
kwise	knitwise
LH	left hand
lp(s)	loop(s)
m	meter(s)
M1	make one—an increase—several increases can be described as "M1"
M1 p-st	make one purl stitch
MC	main color
mm	millimeter(s)
oz	ounce(s)
p or **P**	purl

Abbreviation	Description
pat(s) or **patt**	pattern(s)
pm	place marker
pop	popcorn
p2tog	purl 2 stitches together
prev	previous
psso	pass slipped stitch over
pwise	purlwise
rem	remain/remaining
rep	repeat(s)
rev St st	reverse stockinette stitch
RH	right hand
rnd(s)	round(s)
RS	right side
sk	skip
skp	slip, knit, pass stitch over—one stitch decreased
sk2p	slip 1, knit 2 together, pass slip stitch over the knit 2 together; 2 stitches have been decreased
sl	slip
sl1k	slip 1 knitwise
sl1p	slip 1 purlwise
sl st	slip stitch(es)
ss	slip stitch (Canadian)
ssk	slip, slip, knit these 2 stitches together—a decrease
sssk	slip, slip, slip, knit 3 stitches together
st(s)	stitch(es)
St st	stockinette stitch/stocking stitch
tbl	through back loop
tog	together
WS	wrong side
wyib	with yarn in back
wyif	with yarn in front
yd(s)	yard(s)
yfwd	yarn forward
yo	yarn over
yrn	yarn around needle
yon	yarn over needle

Skill Levels for Knitting

SKILL LEVELS FOR KNITTING

1	■□□□	**Beginner**	Projects for first-time knitters using basic knit and purl stitches. Minimal shaping.
2	■■□□	**Easy**	Projects using basic stitches, repetitive stitch patterns, simple color changes, and simple shaping and finishing.
3	■■■□	**Intermediate**	Projects with a variety of stitches, such as basic cables and lace, simple intarsia, double pointed needles and knitting in the round needle techniques, mid-level shaping and finishing.
4	■■■■	**Experienced**	Projects using advanced techniques and stitches, such as short rows, Fair Isle, more intricate intarsia, cables, lace patterns, and numerous color changes.

Appendices courtesy of the Craft Yarn Council of America www.yarnstandards.com

Standard Body Measurements/Sizing

Most crochet and knitting pattern instructions will provide general sizing information, such as the chest or bust measurements of a completed garment. Many patterns also include detailed schematics or line drawings. These drawings show specific garment measurements (bust/chest, neckline, back, waist, sleeve length, etc.) in all the different pattern sizes. To ensure proper fit, always review all of the sizing information provided in a pattern before you begin.

Following are several sizing charts. These charts show Chest, Center Back Neck-to-Cuff, Back Waist Length, Cross Back, and Sleeve Length **actual body measurements** for babies, children, women, and men. These measurements are given in both inches and centimeters.

When sizing sweaters, the fit is based on actual chest/bust measurements, plus ease (additional inches or centimeters). The first chart entitled "Fit" recommends the amount of ease to add to body measurements if you prefer a close-fitting garment, an oversized garment, or something in-between.

The next charts provide average lengths for children's, women's, and men's garments.

Both the Fit and Length charts are simply guidelines. For individual body differences, changes can be made in body and sleeve lengths when appropriate. However, consideration must be given to the project pattern. Certain sizing changes may alter the appearance of a garment.

HOW TO MEASURE

1. Chest/Bust
Measure around the fullest part of the chest/bust. Do not draw the tape too tightly.

2. Center Back Neck–to-Cuff
With arm slightly bent, measure from back base of neck across shoulder around bend of elbow to wrist.

3. Back Waist Length
Measure from the most prominent bone at base of neck to the natural waistline.

4. Cross Back
Measure from shoulder to shoulder.

5. Sleeve Length
With arm slightly bent, measure from armpit to cuff.

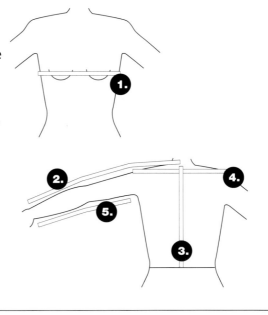

Standard Body Measurements/Sizing continued

FIT

Very-close fitting: Actual chest/bust measurement or less
Close-fitting: 1–2"/2.5–5cm
Standard-fitting: 2–4"/5–10cm
Loose-fitting: 4–6"/10–15cm
Oversized: 6"/15cm or more

LENGTH FOR CHILDREN

Waist length: Actual body measurement
Hip length: 2"/5cm down from waist
Tunic length: 6"/15cm down from waist

LENGTH FOR WOMEN

Waist length: Actual body measurement
Hip length: 6"/15cm down from waist
Tunic length: 11"/28cm down from waist

LENGTH FOR MEN

Men's length usually varies only 1–2"/ 2.5–5cm from the actual "back hip length" measurement (*see chart*)

Baby's size	3 months	6 months	12 months	18 months	24 months
1. Chest (in.)	16	17	18	19	20
(cm.)	40.5	43	45.5	48	50.5
2. Center Back Neck-to-Cuff	10½	11½	12½	14	18
	26.5	29	31.5	35.5	45.5
3. Back Waist Length	6	7	7½	8	8½
	15.5	17.5	19	20.5	21.5
4. Cross Back (Shoulder to Shoulder)	7¼	7¾	8¼	8½	8¾
	18.5	19.5	21	21.5	22
5. Sleeve Length to Underarm	6	6½	7½	8	8½
	15.5	16.5	19	20.5	21.5

Child's size	2	4	6	8	10
1. Chest (in.)	21	23	25	26½	28
(cm.)	53	58.5	63.5	67	71
2. Center Back Neck-to-Cuff	18	19½	20½	22	24
	45.5	49.5	52	56	61
3. Back Waist Length	8½	9½	10½	12½	14
	21.5	24	26.5	31.5	35.5
4. Cross Back (Shoulder to Shoulder)	9¼	9¾	10¼	10¾	11¼
	23.5	25	26	27	28.5
5. Sleeve Length to Underarm	8½	10½	11½	12½	13½
	21.5	26.5	29	31.5	34.5

Standard Body Measurements/Sizing continued

Child's (cont.)	12	14	16
1. Chest (in.)	30	31½	32½
(cm.)	*76*	*80*	*82.5*
2. Center Back Neck-to-Cuff	26 *66*	27 *68.5*	28 *71*
3. Back Waist Length	15 *38*	15½ *39.5*	16 *40.5*
4. Cross Back (Shoulder to Shoulder)	12 *30.5*	12¼ *31*	13 *33*
5. Sleeve Length to Underarm	15 *38*	16 *40.5*	16½ *42*

Woman's size	X-Small	Small	Medium	Large
1. Bust (in.)	28–30	32–34	36–38	40–42
(cm.)	*71–76*	*81–86*	*91.5–96.5*	*101.5–106.5*
2. Center Back Neck-to-Cuff	27–27½ *68.5–70*	28–28½ *71–72.5*	29–29½ *73.5–75*	30–30½ *76–77.5*
3. Back Waist Length	16½ *42*	17 *43*	17¼ *43.5*	17½ *44.5*
4. Cross Back (Shoulder to Shoulder)	14–14½ *35.5–37*	14½–15 *37–38*	16–16½ *40.5–42*	17–17½ *43–44.5*
5. Sleeve Length to Underarm	16½ *42*	17 *43*	17 *43*	17½ *44.5*

Woman's (cont.)	1X	2X	3X	4X	5X
1. Bust (in.)	44–46	48–50	52–54	56–58	60–62
(cm.)	*111.5–117*	*122–127*	*132–137*	*142–147*	*152–158*
2. Center Back Neck-to-Cuff	31–31½ *78.5–80*	31½–32 *80–81.5*	32½–33 *82.5–84*	32½–33 *82.5–84*	33–33½ *84–85*
3. Back Waist Length	17¾ *45*	18 *45.5*	18 *45.5*	18½ *47*	18½ *47*
4. Cross Back (Shoulder to Shoulder)	17½ *44.5*	18 *45.5*	18 *45.5*	18½ *47*	18½ *47*
5. Sleeve Length to Underarm	17½ *44.5*	18 *45.5*	18 *45.5*	18½ *47*	18½ *47*

Standard Body Measurements/Sizing continued

Man's Size	Small	Medium	Large	X-Large	XX-Large
1. Chest (in.)	34–36	38–40	42–44	46–48	50–52
(cm.)	*86–91.5*	*96.5–101.5*	*106.5–111.5*	*116.5–122*	*127–132*
2. Center Back Neck-to-Cuff	32–32½	33–33½	34–34½	35–35½	36–36½
	81–82.5	*83.5–85*	*86.5–87.5*	*89–90*	*91.5–92.5*
3. Back Hip Length	25–25½	26½–26¾	27–27¼	27½–27¾	28–28½
	63.5–64.5	*67.5–68*	*68.5–69*	*69.5–70.5*	*71–72.5*
4. Cross Back (Shoulder to Shoulder)	15½–16	16½–17	17½–18	18–18½	18½–19
	39.5–40.5	*42–43*	*44.5–45.5*	*45.5–47*	*47–48*
5. Sleeve Length to Underarm	18	18½	19½	20	20½
	45.5	*47*	*49.5*	*50.5*	*52*

Head Circumference Chart

	Infant/Child				Adult	
	Premie	**Baby**	**Toddler**	**Child**	**Woman**	**Man**
6. Circumference						
(in.)	12	14	16	18	20	22
(cm.)	*30.5*	*35.5*	*40.5*	*45.5*	*50.5*	*56*

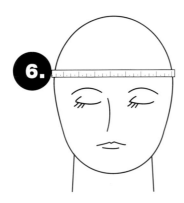

6. For an accurate head measure, place a tape measure across the forehead and measure around the full circumference of the head. Keep the tape snug for accurate results.

Standard Yarn Weight System

Categories of yarn, gauge ranges, and recommended needle and hook sizes

Yarn Weight Symbol & Category Names	**1** Super Fine	**2** Fine	**3** Light	**4** Medium	**5** Bulky	**6** Super Bulky
Type of Yarns in Category	Sock, Fingering, Baby	Sport, Baby	DK, Light Worsted	Worsted, Afghan, Aran	Chunky, Craft, Rug	Bulky, Roving
Knit Gauge Range* in Stockinette Stitch to 4 inches	27–32 sts	23–26 sts	21–24 sts	16–20 sts	12–15 sts	6–11 sts
Recommended Needle in Metric Size Range	2.25–3.25 mm	3.25–3.75 mm	3.75—4.5 mm	4.5–5.5 mm	5.5–8 mm	8 mm and larger
Recommended Needle U.S. Size Range	1 to 3	3 to 5	5 to 7	7 to 9	9 to 11	11 and larger
Crochet Gauge* Ranges in Single Crochet to 4 inch	21–32 sts	16–20 sts	12–17 sts	11–14 sts	8–11 sts	5–9 sts
Recommended Hook in Metric Size Range	2.25–3.5 mm	3.5—4.5 mm	4.5–5.5 mm	5.5–6.5 mm	6.5–9 mm	9 mm and larger
Recommended Hook U.S. Size Range	B–1 to E–4	E–4 to 7	7 to I–9	I–9 to K–10½	K–10½ to M–13	M–13 and larger

* GUIDELINES ONLY: The above reflect the most commonly used gauges and needle or hook sizes for specific yarn categories.

Resources

BOOKS

Berry, Leigh Ann. *Basic Knitting*. Mechanicsburg, PA: Stackpole Books, 2004.

Bliss, Debbie. *How to Knit*. North Pomfret, VT: Trafalgar Square, 1999.

Square, Vicki. *The Knitters Companion*. Loveland, CO: Interweave Press, 1999.

Swansen, Meg. *Handknitting With Meg Swansen*. Pittsville, WI: Schoolhouse Press, 1995.

————. *Meg Swansen's Knitting*. Loveland, CO: Interweave Press, 1999.

Vogue Knitting Magazine Editors. *Vogue Knitting: The Ultimate Knitting Book*. Rev. ed. New York: SoHo Publishing Co., 2002.

Walker, Barbara. *Chart Knitting Designs: A Third Treasury of Knitting Patterns*. Pittsville, WI: Schoolhouse Press, 1998.

————. *A Fourth Treasury of Knitting Patterns*. Pittsville, WI: Schoolhouse Press, 1997.

————. *Mosaic Knitting*. Pittsville, WI: Schoolhouse Press, 1997.

————. *A Second Treasury of Knitting Patterns*. Pittsville, WI: Schoolhouse Press, 1998.

————. *A Treasury of Knitting Patterns*. Pittsville, WI: Schoolhouse, Press, 1998.

Wiseman, Nancie. *The Knitter's Book of Finishing Techniques*. Woodinville, WA: Martingale, 2002.

Zimmerman, Elizabeth. *Elizabeth Zimmerman's Knitter's Almanac*. Mineola, NY: Dover Publications, 1985.

————. *Elizabeth Zimmerman's Knitting Workshop*. Pittsville, WI: Schoolhouse Press, 1989.

————. *Knitting Around*. Pittsville, WI: Schoolhouse Press, 1989.

————. *Knitting Without Tears: Basic Techniques and Easy-to-Follow Directions for Garments to Fit All Sizes*. New York: Simon and Schuster, 1973.

YARN AND KNITTING SUPPLIES

One of the true joys of knitting is finding a good local yarn shop and establishing a relationship with the people who work there. Knitting store employees are almost always knitters themselves and can serve as an invaluable resource, especially for beginners. Most urban areas have at least one good yarn shop. Check your local telephone directory. You can also refer to the wonderful online list compiled at *www.woolworks.org* to find knitting stores in your area.

If you are not fortunate enough to live near a local yarn shop, there are several good online resources and catalogs that you can use. There are hundreds of such retail outlets available on the internet; just a few are mentioned here. Use a search engine such as *www.google.com* to find others.

NOTE: Some online retailers also have brick and mortar stores. Where applicable, a street address is provided.

Halcyon Yarn
12 School Street
Bath, ME 04530
800-341-0282
www.halcyonyarn.com

Kaleidoscope Yarns
15 Pearl Street
Essex Junction, VT 05452
802-288-9200
www.kyarns.com

LeClerc Looms (Fringe Twisters)
819-362-7207
www.leclerclooms.com

PatternWorks
P.O. Box 1618
Center Harbor, NH 03226
800-723-9210
www.patternworks.com

Schoolhouse Press (books and yarn)
800-968-5648
www.schoolhousepress.com

Worldknit.com, Inc.
866-331-5648
www.worldknit.com

ONLINE RESOURCES FOR KNITTERS

ChicKnits
A fun and useful collection of tips, patterns, and links, as well as the author's knitting blog.
www.chicknits.com

Craft Yarn Council of America
The craft yarn industry's trade association website with wonderful educational links and free projects. Link to downloadable version of the Standards and Guidelines for Crochet and Knitting.
www.craftyarncouncil.com

Interweave Press
Publisher of *Interweave Knits* magazine and many great knitting books. Website contains back issues and pattern errata as well as links to knitting charities and other information.
www.interweave.com

Judy Pascale Website
The originator of the twice-worked bind off used in the Lantz Corners Shawl pattern (page 51), Judy is a professional knitting instructor and designer. Her site includes her patterns and class schedule.
www.judypascale.com

KnitPicks Knitting Room
A broad range of knitting topics—from beginner to professional—as well as articles on yarn and other useful subjects. A link to the KnitPicks podcast is also included.
www.knitpicks.com

Knitter's Review
An online magazine with extensive yarn and book review archives as well as patterns and discussion boards.
www.knittersreview.com

The Knitting Guild Association
The national association for hand knitters and publisher of *Cast On* magazine. Website contains membership information and a link to the magazine.
www.tkga.com

The Knitting Universe
Online site for *Knitter's Magazine* and XRX Books. Pattern errata and back issues as well as an online forum and mailing list.
www.knittinguniverse.com

Knitty
A delightful quarterly web-only knitting magazine with articles, columns, and patterns.
www.knitty.com

Vogue Knitting
Publisher of *Vogue Knitting* magazine and many great knitting books. Site includes corrections as well as online access to the current issue of the magazine.
www.vogueknitting.com

Woolworks
The oldest and one of the best collections of hand-knitting information on the internet. A great directory of knitting stores around the world.
www.woolworks.org

Yarn Information

Brown Sheep Company's Lamb's Pride Worsted. (used in most skill workshops and a few Basic Skill Reviews). Visit *http://brownsheep.com* to find a yarn shop near you.

Skacel Merino Light (used throughout the Basic Skills Review). Visit *www.skacelknitting.com* to find a yarn shop near you.

Wool in the Woods (used in all sample projects).

Several of the Wool in the Woods yarns used in the sample projects are no longer available. Please contact Cherry Tree Hill Yarns at (800) 525-3311 for availability or advice on yarn substitution. Visit *www.cherryyarn.com* for more information.